STRESSES IN U.S.-JAPANESE
SECURITY RELATIONS

FRED GREENE

STRESSES IN U.S.-JAPANESE
SECURITY RELATIONS

THE BROOKINGS INSTITUTION
Washington, D.C.

Library of Congress Cataloging in Publication Data:

Greene, Fred.
   Stresses in U.S.-Japanese security relations.
   (Studies in defense policy)
   Includes bibliographical references.
   1. Japan—Foreign relations—United States.
2. United States—Foreign relations—Japan. 3. Military
assistance, American—Japan. I. Title. II. Series.
E183.8.J3G714   327.52′073   75-4421
ISBN 0-8157-3271-6 pbk.

9 8 7 6 5 4 3 2 1

THE BROOKINGS INSTITUTION is an independent organization devoted to nonpartisan research, education, and publication in economics, government, foreign policy, and the social sciences generally. Its principal purposes are to aid in the development of sound public policies and to promote public understanding of issues of national importance.

The Institution was founded on December 8, 1927, to merge the activities of the Institute for Government Research, founded in 1916, the Institute of Economics, founded in 1922, and the Robert Brookings Graduate School of Economics and Government, founded in 1924.

The Board of Trustees is responsible for the general administration of the Institution, while the immediate direction of the policies, program, and staff is vested in the President, assisted by an advisory committee of the officers and staff. The by-laws of the Institution state: "It is the function of the Trustees to make possible the conduct of scientific research, and publication, under the most favorable conditions, and to safeguard the independence of the research staff in the pursuit of their studies and in the publication of the results of such studies. It is not a part of their function to determine, control, or influence the conduct of particular investigations or the conclusions reached."

The President bears final responsibility for the decision to publish a manuscript as a Brookings book. In reaching his judgment on the competence, accuracy, and objectivity of each study, the President is advised by the director of the appropriate research program and weighs the views of a panel of expert outside readers who report to him in confidence on the quality of the work. Publication of a work signifies that it is deemed a competent treatment worthy of public consideration but does not imply endorsement of conclusions or recommendations.

The Institution maintains its position of neutrality on issues of public policy in order to safeguard the intellectual freedom of the staff. Hence interpretations or conclusions in Brookings publications should be understood to be solely those of the authors and should not be attributed to the Institution, to its trustees, officers, or other staff members, or to the organizations that support its research.

FOREWORD

Important trends and events—notably the end of the war in Indochina, the revival of Japanese economic power, the U.S. rapprochement with China, and détente between the Soviet Union and the United States—have drastically altered the international environment of the mutual security treaty signed by the United States and Japan more than twenty years ago. Although the maintenance of a close U.S.-Japanese security tie remains a key objective of both governments, these changed circumstances pose difficult questions about the function of the security treaty and of U.S. military bases in Japan.

This study discusses the principal questions at issue, particularly among the Japanese, concerning the treaty and the bases. The author also analyzes Japan's own defense program and the problems of coordinating it with U.S. security policies in northeast Asia. He concludes with specific recommendations for changes in U.S. and Japanese policies that he considers desirable to ensure that bilateral security arrangements receive domestic political support and continue to serve the needs of both countries over the next five years.

Fred Greene carried out this study as a senior fellow in the Brookings Foreign Policy Studies program while on leave of absence from Williams College. He is grateful to Ralph Clough of the Brookings Institution, many of whose suggestions are incorporated in the manuscript, and to Goddard W. Winterbottom, who edited it.

The Institution acknowledges the assistance of the Ford Foundation for its grants in support of defense and foreign policy studies. The views expressed are those of the author and should not be attributed to the Ford Foundation or the trustees, officers, or other staff members of the Brookings Institution.

KERMIT GORDON
President

January 1975
Washington, D.C.

vii

CONTENTS

CHAPTER ONE

INTRODUCTION

It is difficult to know whether to emphasize the uniqueness of a trans-Pacific security alliance that has lasted for more than twenty years or to concentrate on challenges that have beset it almost from the outset. The U.S.-Japanese mutual security treaty (MST) has a remarkable record for both endurance and stress and promises to continue along this strange dual track well into the future. From the beginning, its Japanese advocates saw clear advantages: security against powerful communist military challenges, an end to the occupation of the home islands and eventually of Okinawa, economic assistance and cooperation, and above all good relations with a powerful former enemy. Internally the arrangement spared Japan the economic burden of rearming and helped keep the dominant conservative regime from adopting more militant policies.[1]

Yet from the outset, as the Socialist party (JSP) took a strong stand against alignment and national self-defense, opposition also was intense. This antagonism has continued unabated, in contrast to the situation in European states, in which a consensus to accept NATO emerged within the noncommunist parties of West Germany, Italy, and other nations during the 1950s. Nor has the treaty ever been accepted in a positive sense by the Japanese public; rather, it generally has been regarded as at best a necessary evil.[2] Moreover, antagonism to the U.S. force and base presence has grown, especially as Japan has recovered its economic

1. Morton Halperin, "U.S.-Japanese Security Relations," paper prepared for Japanese-American seminar, January 1973; Shinkichi Etō, "Increasing Japan's Security Capabilities," *Journal of Social and Political Ideas of Japan* (hereafter *JSPIJ*), vol. 4 (August 1966), pp. 38–42.

2. See, for example, the strong anti-American tone in Moriteru Arasaki, "Okinawa's Reversion and the Security of Japan," *Japan Interpreter*, vol. 6 (Autumn 1970), pp. 281–93. A few years earlier, the editors of *JSPIJ* summarized critical views by Yoshikazu Sakamoto and Toshiyuki Toyoda in a symposium in *Ekonomisuto* (October 1965); see *JSPIJ*, vol. 4 (April 1966), p. 40. See also Hiroharu Seki, "Systems of Power Balance and the Preservation of Peace," *JSPIJ*, vol. 5 (April 1967), pp. 43–63.

strength and as the Sino-Soviet split has made a direct threat only a somewhat remote possibility. Always believing that the U.S. military installations served American rather than Japanese interests and strongly against any Japanese involvement in anyone else's security problems, the opponents of the bases intensified their efforts during the Vietnam war.[3] They stressed the linkage between the bases and a war that most Japanese considered morally unacceptable, politically unwise for the United States, and capable of involving them in a conflict with China. And more recently the general impact of U.S.-Chinese détente has led opponents to shift their ground from criticizing the MST as a danger to challenging it as unnecessary.

In its specific provisions, the Treaty of Mutual Cooperation and Security of 1960 commits the United States to assist in the defense of Japan and gives it the right to maintain bases and other facilities in Japan, not only for the defense of that country but also for the maintenance of international peace and security in the Far East. Unlike the mutual defense treaties between the United States and other nations of the western Pacific, the U.S.-Japanese security treaty does not obligate the Japanese to respond if U.S. territories or forces in the Pacific area should be attacked. It commits Japan only to defense of its own territories, acknowledging implicitly that the Japanese constitution forbids the use of the nation's forces elsewhere. By an exchange of notes accompanying the treaty, the United States agreed that major changes in the deployment of U.S. forces into Japan, major changes in their equipment, and the use of facilities and areas in Japan as bases for combat operations elsewhere would be the subjects of prior consultation with the Japanese government.

In addition to its security provisions, the treaty provides that the United States and Japan will seek to eliminate mutual conflict in their international economic policies and to encourage economic collaboration. After its first ten-year period, the treaty continues in force indefinitely, but may be abrogated by either party with one year's notice.

Under provisions of the treaty eight major military installations in Japan proper, five of them in the Tokyo area, are either under U.S. control or available to be shared with the Japanese Self-Defense Force.

---

3. For a balanced discussion of the problem of autonomy, see Saburō Hayashi, "Autonomous Diplomacy and Defense," *JSPIJ*, vol. 2 (August 1964), pp. 100–03. The development of a negative view toward the security treaty is argued in Etō, "Increasing," pp. 42–47. On Vietnam, see F. Roy Lockheimer, "Vietnam Through a Japanese Mirror," American University Field Staff East Asian Series, vol. 16, no. 7 (April 1969).

Even more extensive U.S. bases and facilities occupy some 75,000 acres in Okinawa. This large base complex was relied on heavily to support U.S. military operations in Vietnam. Over the years, the two governments periodically have reached agreements to reduce U.S. installations in Japan, a recent instance being a consolidation agreement in 1973.

Article IX of the American-drafted Japanese constitution provides not only that the Japanese people "forever renounce war" and "the threat or use of force as a means of settling international disputes," but also that "land, sea, and air forces, as well as other war potential, will never be maintained." The Japanese Supreme Court has ruled, however, that Japan has the same inherent right of self-defense as any sovereign nation, and that these constitutional provisions do not prevent the maintenance of defensive forces. The protection afforded by the security treaty and the presence of U.S. forces in Japan have permitted the Japanese to maintain a relatively small defense force, one of 240,000 men armed with conventional weapons only. By 1976, upon completion of the fourth defense buildup plan, Japan will have a small elite force with modern aircraft, warships, and other weapons, some of them produced in Japan. But this force will not be strong enough to defend Japan against a large-scale conventional attack without U.S. help, and none of its weapons will be able to project Japanese power abroad. A few Japanese have advocated the acquisition of nuclear weapons, but the bulk of the Japanese people firmly support the "three nuclear principles" proclaimed by the Japanese government—that Japan will neither manufacture nor possess nuclear weapons and will not permit them to be located in Japan.

Despite strong continuing opposition within Japan, the bilateral security relation has proved remarkably durable. But it remains subject to a variety of stresses, rooted not only in the long-standing split within Japanese domestic politics but also in developments of the 1960s and early 1970s, particularly the resurgence of Japanese self-confidence and economic power and the new uncertainties created by America détente diplomacy. The primary strategic imbalance that gave rise to the alliance remains: a lightly armed Japan with two powerful communist neighbors. But the Sino-Soviet dispute reduces the likelihood of strong military pressure against Japan by either antagonist. At the same time, the U.S. overtures to the two communist powers have increased Japanese anxiety about the credibility of American security guarantees should such pressure arise, particularly since the opening toward China in 1971 was accomplished with such secrecy and suddenness. And Japanese of many political persuasions, united in favoring an autonomous diplomacy less dependent on the United States (and in feeling that a country whose postwar achievements are so substantial ought to pursue a more independent policy course), are uncertain and divided about the directions such a diplomacy should take and how fast it should proceed.

This study seeks both to explore these general issues and to describe in some detail how the postwar defense relation has worked in practice. It begins, in Chapter Two, with an exploration of the security debate in Japan, based not only on published sources but on numerous interviews—with persons inside and outside government—in Tokyo during the summer of 1972. In Chapter Three the discussion focuses on the bilateral security treaty and the specific problems that have arisen in its implementation. These include its application to the defense of third countries in the region, as well as issues of American troop deployment and base structure. Chapter Four covers the question of Japan's own defense capabilities, combining a general discussion of Japanese defense policy and attitudes with specific information about the evolution of the Self-Defense Force. Chapter Five presents the author's recommendations about how specific issues can be handled so as to ease the stresses that will inevitably continue to arise.

Obviously, Japan is experiencing many contradictory pulls, which intensify ambivalent attitudes among officials, nonofficial experts, and the general public. The forces behind maintenance of security ties are considerable, yet a substantial alteration in U.S.-Japanese security relations is not out of the question. Juxtaposed to the desire for autonomy is a hesitation to go it alone and a fear of reduced American ties; and juxtaposed to the security value and possible manipulative value of the Sino-Soviet split are the potential dangers caused by this rupture. Regionally, other Asian states want an active Japanese presence, in economic aid and as a counterweight to China, but at the same time they fear Tokyo's domination. General opposition in Japan to an extensive rearmament program combines with a widespread expectation that this will eventually come to pass. Finally and most confusing of all, the Japanese want to reduce the U.S. military presence, yet they fear a complete pullout and strategic disengagement from the western Pacific by the United States.

Against this background, we shall consider the security debate in Japan and how recent events have affected it.

CHAPTER TWO

THE SECURITY DEBATE IN JAPAN

The continuing debate in Japan over security relations with the United States covers a variety of issues. Some are of long standing; others are products of the thawing of the cold war in general and the new relation with mainland China in particular. This chapter begins with a brief discussion of major Japanese security problems and the internal dialogue they have generated. It will then treat, at greater length, two issues that have raised concern in Japan: the reliability of the American security commitment in the wake of the "Nixon shocks" of 1971 (both diplomatic and economic), and the degree to which the treaty relation is consistent with the widespread Japanese desire for greater autonomy and innovation in its foreign policy. It closes with an analysis of the constraining impact of domestic politics on the security policies that postwar conservative governments have pursued.

General Issues

The central issue in the Japanese debate over the security treaty is whether its value to Japan outweighs its disadvantages. Opponents of the treaty argue that it serves primarily U.S. purposes. They often focus their attack on the so-called Far East clause, which gives the United States the right to use bases in Japan for maintaining peace and security elsewhere in the Far East. They deny that the USSR or mainland China poses any threat to Japan and charge that the treaty, instead of making Japan more secure, actually creates the danger that Japan might be dragged into a war by the United States. Critics who accept the need for the treaty accuse the Japanese government of interpreting its provisions in ways too favorable to the United States; they point out that the prior consultation requirement has never been invoked despite extensive use of U.S. facilities in Japan to support U.S. military operations in Vietnam.

U.S. bases and facilities in Japan are prime targets of treaty opponents because it is easier to arouse public opposition to them than to the treaty itself. The bases are unpleasant reminders of the U.S. military occupation of Japan, and they occupy valuable land in some of Japan's most crowded areas. Operations from the bases add to already severe problems of traffic congestion and air and noise pollution. A growing body of opinion in Japan would have U.S. forces withdraw from Japan, to return only to answer a threat that clearly required their presence.

The Japanese generally agree on the need for the Japanese Self-Defense Force, although the Japanese Socialist party (JSP), which advocates unarmed neutrality for Japan, argues that the SDF is unconstitutional. Important differences remain, however, over the distinction between offensive and defensive weapons and between those who would develop a stronger force than is projected under the fourth defense buildup plan and those who argue that the plan should be cut back.

In the nuclear field, whether Japan should have nuclear weapons is not seriously debated; current debate centers on whether Japan should ratify the nuclear nonproliferation treaty or keep open its option to produce nuclear weapons if international conditions should change. The change that would have the strongest bearing on these issues would be a decline in the credibility of the U.S. defense commitment to Japan.

From the strictly military view, Japan faced—and still must consider—both the Soviet capacity for a nuclear strike and China's increasing capability to launch a strategic attack with medium- to intermediate-range missiles. The USSR also has the capability for a massive conventional attack, against which Japan has concentrated over one-third of its defense force in the north; by contrast, China lacks the air and sea power for this type of threat. The USSR and, to a lesser degree, China could harass Japan's vulnerable sea lanes of communication and transportation, a threat that the U.S. accord, the naval bases, and the presence of the Seventh Fleet now effectively minimize.[1]

Furthermore, the Japanese have been keenly sensitive to a danger to their internal security that would be sparked by a North Korean takeover of the entire Korean peninsula, and in the early 1960s certain contingency plans dealt with that possibility.[2] A new Korean war also

1. See the formal presentation by Under Secretary of State U. Alexis Johnson in *United States Security Agreements and Commitments Abroad: Japan and Okinawa*, Hearings before the Subcommittee on U.S. Security Agreements and Commitments Abroad of the Senate Committee on Foreign Relations, 91 Cong. 2 sess. (January 26–29, 1970), pp. 1417–18, and his response to interrogations, pp. 1207–09.
2. On the Three Arrows Plan controversy during the mid-1960s, regarding

would generate foreign uncertainties, including the possible participation of the major powers, with the implied dangers of escalation. Again, the American security link, together with the U.S. defense commitment to Seoul, offer considerable reassurance. In general, Japanese analysts have observed that general war did not break out between cold war alliance blocs in the generation after 1945. They conclude that participation in a defense accord with the United States undoubtedly contributed to their country's success in avoiding war, especially in light of the armed conflicts that affected various nonaligned states during that time.

Even strong opponents of the mutual security treaty during the past decade recognize its earlier value to the balance of power and to Japan, especially through America's naval power.[3] The MST also increased Tokyo's psychological assurance at a time of great uneasiness. It contributed heavily to the country's speedy economic growth by minimizing the domestic defense burden and helped prevent a more militant anticommunist regime from coming to power in Tokyo.[4]

Critics argued during the 1960s, however, that the MST had become a danger to Japan because it was unnecessarily provocative to an otherwise peace-oriented China. In addition, by permitting establishment of the U.S. bases, Japan risked becoming a target of reprisal for American military action against communist interests on the mainland, as in Vietnam. Critics feared also that the United States would not effectively prevent an enemy from inflicting an unacceptable amount of damage on Japan. The critics added that the collective defense arrangements of the cold war era tended to intensify hostilities between governments and the people in politically unstable areas and thereby threatened to convert civil conflicts into international wars.[5]

---

contingency plans for internal security in Japan in case of an outbreak of war in Korea, see Matsueda Tsukasa and George E. Moore, "Japan's Shifting Attitude toward the Military: *Mitsuyu Kenkyū* and the Self-Defense Force," *Asian Survey*, vol. 7 (September 1967), pp. 614–25; and Martin E. Weinstein, *Japan's Postwar Defense Policy 1947–1968* (Columbia University Press, 1971), p. 173. The recent draft strategic doctrine notes that a Chinese threat would also take the form of an internal insurgency: *New York Times*, March 4, 1973.

3. Masataka Kōsaka, "Japan as a Maritime Nation," in *Journal of Social and Political Ideas of Japan* (hereafter *JSPIJ*), vol. 3 (August 1965), pp. 49–56.

4. Shinkichi Etō, "Increasing Japan's Security Capabilities," *JSPIJ*, vol. 4 (August 1966), pp. 38–42.

5. Articles by Yoshikazu Sakamoto and Toshiyuki Toyoda as summarized by the editors, *JSPIJ*, vol. 4 (April 1966). For an earlier anti-alliance presentation, see Sakamoto, "A Defense Plan for a Neutral Japan," summarized from *Sekai* (August 1959), *JSPIJ*, vol. 4 (April 1966), p. 41.

In light of recent changes in the international politics of Asia, the content of such criticism altered dramatically, yet its intensity has remained or even increased. U.S. and Japanese détente with China, the Sino-Soviet split, and the efforts of the two Koreas to come to terms have led opponents to argue that the treaty is now unnecessary rather than dangerous, an encumbrance on Japan's quest for independence and a more flexible foreign policy. In fact, because the focus of danger—in day-to-day diplomacy though not in deployment of Japanese forces—had shifted from the USSR to China during the 1960s, the normalization of relations between Peking and Tokyo was alleged to have ended any rationale for the treaty. Such an argument had considerable appeal to a public that was generally uneasy about the accord and willing to live with it only because no alternative emerged.

But the advocates of retaining the MST even in an era of détente have been able to muster a response. Recognizing the unacceptability of war to Japan, defense officials and others stressed deterrence as the treaty's main role and argued that actually this always had been its main justification.[6] Achievement of this deterrence, as well as the MST's contribution to the balance of power in Asia, had permitted the understandings with Peking in the first place, and only its continuation could sustain the détente and keep both communist states from adopting less benign policies. Furthermore, the Tanaka government held, the arguments that the MST would make Japan anathema to China or that the United States would prevent a Tokyo-Peking accord now had been proved totally incorrect.[7]

The Tanaka visit to Peking in 1972 demonstrated that Japan enjoyed flexibility in its foreign policy and that the MST may actually have strengthened Tokyo's hand. The fact that it proved no obstacle to the Sino-Japanese settlement went so deeply against the understanding of the opposition parties, immersed as they were in their own cold war imagery, that they could not adjust readily to the new turn of events. It can even be argued that the MST, as well as Tanaka's commitment regarding Taiwan in Honolulu in mid-1972, mollified the Liberal Democratic party (LDP) hawks sufficiently to clear the way for his accord with Peking that September. Tanaka later defended the MST forcefully, arguing that it was not an anachronistic holdover from the cold war era. He

6. Takuya Kubo, "Revaluation of Japan-U.S. Security Treaty," written in April 1972 for the June 1972 issue of *Kokubō*, p. 1. (Page numbers refer to manuscript in English translation received by the author. Kubo is chief of the important Defense Bureau in the Japan Defense Agency.)

7. Foreign Minister Ohira in the Diet, November 10, 1972.

also denied that the China settlement made it obsolete, inasmuch as Japan still lacked the means to defend itself.[8]

In addition, many Japanese scholars have observed that public criticism of the treaty from the USSR has been muted for some years and that during 1972 Chinese opposition decreased sharply and then all but disappeared. They conclude that China wants the MST to continue as part of the power balance in Asia, so essential to hold Moscow in check. They point out also that the Nixon doctrine—which is acceptable to Peking because it implies a U.S. pullback from a forward position in Asia and from a U.S.-Chinese confrontation, without abandoning American interests in the region—depends significantly on the system of U.S. alliances, in which the MST is a crucial factor and therefore acceptable to the Chinese. Such opinions gained added credence following press reports of Chou En-lai's support of a larger Japanese defense effort—and, by inference, of the MST—in his discussions with Prime Minister Tanaka and other political figures in 1972, in order to maintain a balance against the Soviet threat in Asia.[9] Given the proclivity of the Japanese press to echo criticism from abroad, acceptance of the treaty elsewhere in Asia as a stabilizing force in regional affairs well might reduce its significance in Japanese politics.

Such an expectation, however, may be too saguine. Buoyed by its election gains in late 1972, the opposition, especially the Communist party, is proud of its nationalist-independent course—although the main source of its strength actually is LDP weakness in handling domestic problems, particularly urban and economic issues.[10] Opposition parties will continue to stress attractive domestic issues, but they will continue as well their

8. Television interview, October 25, 1972. See also *New York Times,* October 29, 1972; and Tanaka's statement in the Diet, November 10, 1972.

9. See particularly the article by William Beecher, "Chou Is Said to Have Given Japan Military Assurances," *New York Times,* December 14, 1972. The report that Chou also said that Peking might have occasion to aid Japan in case of attack was denied promptly by Cabinet Secretary S. Nikaidō, *New York Times,* December 15, 1972.

10. The election of December 1972 proved a setback for Tanaka and the LDP. Their strength, including that of independents, dropped from 297 to 282, leaving them with 10 fewer seats than they expected to win. The Communist party (JCP) made a spectacular gain, from 14 to 38, and the JSP partially recovered from its low of 90, suffered in the 50-seat loss of 1969, to reach 117: *New York Times,* December 11 and 12, 1972. Opposition candidates also did well in municipal elections. A socialist triumph in Nagoya in April 1973 gave the opposition control of Japan's five largest cities. Later, however, the LDP made a comeback in some municipalities. It could well be argued that the voting pattern of recent years indicated a general erosion of LDP support rather than an increase in opposition strength.

opportunistic exploitation of the issue of U.S. bases, as they did in mid-1972. They still hope to parlay sentiment into an attack on the MST and even to move on from there to their ultimate objective: the challenge of Japan's indigenous defense effort.

Moreover, a public that never has fully grasped the value of the MST will find justification for it even less convincing in an era of détente (despite Peking's recent reversal of attitude), partly because the treaty has been so effective in reducing the likelihood of a Soviet threat to Japan. Japanese officials liken the MST to air and water: of crucial importance but easily taken for granted, its benefits not appreciated. They also express dismay that the populace cannot understand the fluidity of international politics: how quickly—in the absence of a strong guarantee such as the MST—a seemingly secure situation can deteriorate. In addition, concern exists about increased isolationist sentiment in the United States, which adds to fears at play in Japan since the advent of the Nixon doctrine:[11] fear that the United States is turning in on itself, that it expects others to carry a far greater share of the burden, that it will be less likely to intervene in a crisis, that if it does respond there will be less stress on military aspects, that it will give higher priority to responses in Europe than in Asia, and that the importance of the immediate issue rather than whether the state is an ally will determine whether the United States acts.[12]

These fears, as well as continued agitation by the opposition against the U.S. tie and the LDP's uncertain posture in dealing with defense matters, all point to continuing difficulties.[13] At the same time, the end of

11. Kubo, "Revaluation," p. 3.

12. Continuing strains in ongoing bilateral U.S.-Japanese relations added to the difficulties, and evidences of that condition remained plentiful. Foreign Minister Ohira expressed his concern over U.S. treatment of Japan: *New York Times,* January 26, 1973. Japan expressed its dismay over not being included in the arrangements for Vietnam at the time of Kissinger's visit to Tokyo: *New York Times,* February 19 and 20, 1973. LDP Secretary General T. Hashimoto denounced the fact that Japan was not consulted about a settlement in Indochina: *New York Times,* February 20, 1973. Finally, the cancellation of the emperor's visit to the United States was still another symptom indicating continuing bilateral difficulties: *New York Times,* April 25–29, 1973. A thoughtful, balanced analysis of the strains in U.S. relations, reflecting Japan's own uncertainties about its national aspirations, as well as objective difficulties in bilateral ties, can be found in J. A. A. Stockwin, "Continuity of Change in Japanese Foreign Policy," *Pacific Affairs,* vol. 46 (Spring 1973), pp. 77–93.

13. The question of the LDP posture on defense is long standing. On Novem-

the Vietnam war and the improved position of both the United States and Japan in relation to the major communist powers should make the treaty a less visible target. To the extent that obvious threats against Japan remain slight over the next decade, the MST's value increasingly will be that of a "static policy against potential threats" rather than a dynamic response to obvious challenges.[14] This may make its retention less of an immediate operational problem—although continually more difficult to justify in terms of felt security needs. But as already noted, the dramatic foreign policy actions of the Nixon administration multiplied Japanese fear about the actual dependability of the United States as an ally.

Reliability of the U.S. Commitment

The "Nixon shocks" of 1971—the announcement of President Nixon's intention to visit Peking and his suspension of convertibility of the dollar —intensified the uncertainty in Japan about the durability of U.S. concern for Asia, the constancy and continuity of U.S. policy, and the degree to which the United States, despite its verbal reassurances, actually values Japan. Although many Japanese viewed the Nixon visit to Peking as a constructive step that opened the way for a Sino-Japanese rapprochement, it caused much ill will and uncertainty in Japan.[15] The socialists saw in it proof that the United States behaves unpredictably and selfishly. Many conservatives complained that Japan had subserviently followed the U.S. policy of aloofness toward China, only to be duped and left in the lurch, to the embarrassment of the pro-American cabinet of Prime Minister Satō. The U.S. initiative therefore shook Japanese confidence in American credibility and bred confusion about the

---

ber 18, 1964, the LDP Security Research Council recommended a vigorous campaign to enhance public acceptance and understanding of a stronger defense posture and the MST. See Kei Wakaizumi, "Chinese Nuclear Armament and the Security of Japan," *JSPIJ*, vol. 4 (December 1966). Tanaka's more forthright stand in the fall of 1972 may not have been a cause of the December election setback, but the fact that his party lost ground was not likely to lead him to sustain an outspoken position on what evidently is not an advantageous political issue.

14. Kubo, "Revaluation," p. 13.

15. The effect of the combined China and economic shocks of 1971 are described in Lee Farnsworth, "Japan: The Year of the Shock," *Asian Survey,* vol. 12 (January 1972), pp. 48–52.

common-enemy thesis, which had been featured as recently as 1969 in the important Satō-Nixon talks and communiqué.[16]

New Asian Role of the United States

To the Japanese public, the entire security system now appeared doubly doubtful, a feeling that considerably increased the government's difficulty in adhering to established policy. Even those Japanese diplomatic officials who sympathized with the U.S. strategy for peace—a strategy involving a correct if limited friendship with Peking—lost a clear view of U.S. security policy in Asia. They feared that expansion of relations between Washington and Peking conceivably could reduce Japan's value for the United States and lead to more restricted lateral relations or even to mounting U.S.-Japanese antagonism.

Paralleling the new China policy, reduction of U.S. forces in Asia raised doubts about the durability of U.S. security commitments to that region. America's willingness to act in a future ground war became suspect because of both the experience in Vietnam and the emphasis of the Nixon doctrine on indigenous self-defense. By extension, the credibility of the U.S. nuclear deterrent also became clouded.[17]

With economic friction between Japan and the United States on the rise, leftist parties easily were able to adopt a nationalist line and play up a negative image of the United States that drew on the Vietnam war, crime, racial tension, and economic problems. The socialists argued that, in the new climate of détente, the need for a security link with so uncer-

16. For an interesting discussion of U.S.-Japanese difficulties in the aftermath of the "Nixon shocks" from policy and bureaucratic perspectives, see Graham T. Allison, "American Foreign Policy and Japan," in Henry Rosovsky (ed.), *Discord in the Pacific* (Columbia Books, 1972), pp. 10–20. Repercussions in the press and the background of these difficulties are discussed by George Packard, "A Crisis in Understanding," in the same volume.

17. The Nixon doctrine states that the United States "will keep all its treaty commitments" and "provide a shield if a nuclear power threatens the freedom of a nation allied with us" (*United States Foreign Policy for the 1970s, Message from The President of the United States*, 91 Cong. 2 sess. [February 18, 1970], p. 55). But the Japanese and certain American analysts misinterpreted this statement as a commitment only in case the threat involved nuclear weapons and inferred that the United States would expect its Asian allies to handle other military threats by themselves. See John K. Emmerson, *Arms, Yen and Power: The Japanese Dilemma* (Dunellen, 1971), p. 392. Hideo Yamamuro discusses the possible withdrawal of U.S. ground forces from Asia under the Nixon doctrine in "International Situation Surrounding Japan" (speech delivered at the Tokyo Bankers' Club, July 4, 1972; processed).

tain an ally was gone and that the link should be ended. The Communist party (JCP) went one step further: it denounced the U.S.-China accord of February 1972 as lacking an ideological basis and adopted a nationalist position critical of all three major powers.

Successful American and Japanese negotiations with the communist powers, by reducing the threat, undoubtedly have made the security system more difficult to sustain. Foreign Ministry officials expressed the view that the long dormant pacifist-neutralist views of the Socialist party might gain support in the new environment of détente.[18] Together, the successful U.S. efforts in the strategic arms limitation talks, improved relations with China, talks between the two Koreas, and the Vietnam cease-fire strengthened the antialignment argument. Some scholars argued that, as in the period following the Korean war, settlement of the Indochina conflict would lead to a general reduction of tensions, as well as to accommodations among the major powers that could minimize the impact of future tensions. The issue in Japan could be stated simply as "détente versus deterrence," with the alleged primacy of the former making the latter, as exemplified by the MST, seem an unnecessary impediment.[19]

Prospects of a Multipolar International System

The expectation that détente probably will become more firmly established in the new era of multipolarity has led Japanese scholars and defense experts to argue also that antagonism between Washington and Tokyo can best be reduced in a multilateral context, one in which Japan's heavy reliance on the United States for security is diminished. They have taken the view that a general détente could make the MST more acceptable if the treaty were shown to contribute to such a reduction. But the price would be a blurring of existing clear-cut mutual secu-

18. A general review of difficulties in bilateral security relations, centering on the U.S. need to sustain a more forthcoming policy in order to dissuade Japan from following an independent course, is developed by Zbigniew Brzezinski, *The Fragile Blossom* (Harper and Row, 1972). He discusses the point more briefly in "Japan's Global Engagement," *Foreign Affairs*, vol. 50 (January 1972), pp. 270–79.

19. Junnosuke Kishida argues against reliance on a deterrent policy on the grounds that this implies a status quo arrangement, which may be proper for the industrial states but is not applicable to the fluid situation prevalent in the underdeveloped context of East Asia: "Non-Nuclear Japan: Her National Security and Role for Peace in Asia" (paper prepared for Peace in Asia conference, Kyoto, Japan, June 1972; processed).

rity commitments, particularly the U.S. military guarantee and the Japanese provision of bases and facilities in return.

In fact, the idea of a new five-power multipolar era—involving the United States, the USSR, China, Japan, and the European Economic Community—attracted considerable attention in Japan after being aired by President Nixon in 1971. Although it opened the way for a more autonomous foreign policy, the concept generated uneasiness. Presidential foreign policy adviser Henry Kissinger gave repeated assurances over the next two years that it did not signify a weakening of the U.S. security tie and that the President was referring to five economic poles (the two superpowers remaining the bipolar centers of military strength); but his efforts failed to remove Japanese concern. Some Japanese foreign policy experts favor the multipolar idea, holding that détente and military stalemate increase the significance of economic and political strength. In such a world, Japan would weigh heavily because of its economic strength, its expanding capacity for international trade and investment, and its strong role in international monetary affairs.[20] And to a certain degree all five power centers have something in common—a stake in maintaining at least certain aspects of the status quo.

Other Japanese, including some defense officials, reject the idea of five power centers, pointing to the inequality between the superpowers and the others, especially Japan, which alone lacks nuclear weapons. Moreover, Japan's economy relies heavily on an international base that it cannot control—again, in contrast to the other four, which could more closely approach economic independence. Nor could Japan become a major pole by leadership of a regional coalition, because of the absence of strong partners, the distances involved, the great gap in development between Japan and the other countries in the area, and their inevitable suspicion of Japan's intentions.[21]

In addition, some Japanese academic experts are unhappy about the implication of the five-pole concept that Japan should carry a much

20. For a cautious but optimistic projection of Japan's capacity to play a major role in world affairs without military power, see Kei Wakaizumi, "Japan's Role in a New World Order," *Foreign Affairs,* vol. 51 (January 1973), pp. 310–26.

21. For a perceptive view of the regional aspects of multipolar considerations, see Alistair Buchan, "Power Relationships in the Far East: A European View," *Survival,* vol. 14 (May–June 1972), pp. 106–13. For an earlier appraisal, see Coral Bell, "The Asian Power Balance," *Adelphi Papers,* no. 44 (London: International Institute for Strategic Studies, 1968). Kiichi Saeki is critical of the five-pole concept and concludes that Japan remains dependent on the United States for its security: "Japan's Security in a Multipolar World," *Adelphi Papers,* no. 92 (IISS, 1972), pp. 21–29.

greater burden for maintaining world order, in both military security and economic development—particularly in East Asia. This could bring about more serious confrontations with China and, if carried to its logical conclusion, could require a nuclear capability.[22] They are concerned also that the American approach implies equal treatment of the other four poles, with little distinction between its allies and its rivals. This concern has grown as a consequence of Washington's agreements with Moscow and Peking in 1972 and 1973 and of the air of hostility permeating U.S. economic relations with Western Europe and Japan.

Potential Redirection of U.S. Military Strength

The inevitable questioning of U.S. military credibility in such an unsettled diplomatic-security context is directed at both the conventional force and the more publicized nuclear umbrella.

REDUCTIONS IN MILITARY FORCE AND PRESENCE. The Nixon doctrine and U.S. budget cuts after 1969 led to a reduction in facilities in Japan and to proposals, later dropped, for even more significant cutbacks, notably reversion of the Yokosuka naval base. Reduction of U.S. force strength in Taiwan, Korea, and Japan itself in the early 1970s led many Japanese defense experts, inside and outside the government, to conclude that the United States would withdraw completely from Japan. Since then, a tapering off in force reduction and an emphasis on a continued American presence have allayed these concerns somewhat, but suspicion remains that another large-scale withdrawal will occur. Japanese defense officials believe that such an American decision would rest less on an estimate of the Asian situation and more on such considerations as the shortage of combat manpower with the end of the draft, a budgetary squeeze, continued balance-of-payments constraints, and a general determination to concentrate on domestic affairs.

These officials also recognize that the United States will do its utmost to avoid involvement in future Asian ground wars, perhaps even in Japan itself—because, these officials believe, the United States does not consider the home islands to be as important strategically as they were

22. See Chalmers Johnson, "How China and Japan See Each Other," *Foreign Affairs*, vol. 50 (July 1972), pp. 711–21. Yamamuro, in "International Situation," discusses the five-power idea, considers it erroneous, and concludes that we live in a bipolar (U.S.-USSR) structure, with China ranking third, followed by Western Europe and Japan.

during the height of the cold war and before the Sino-Soviet split. Troop withdrawals reinforce their doubts.[23]

Such concern is reinforced also by pressure from within Japan to reduce or eliminate the presence of U.S. troops and their supporting base systems. To some extent, a vicious circle has developed. If one has no faith in American credibility, the U.S. force presence has little justification. Should pressures against a continued American presence induce new withdrawals, the credibility of American support against a conventional Soviet threat, which admittedly is unlikely, would fall even farther.[24]

The U.S. base system in Japan generally is recognized as supportive to other security obligations in East Asia. An American decision to reduce its military presence in Japan drastically during the next few years —by 50 percent, for example—from 1973–74 levels also would raise doubts among other Asian allies about the U.S. commitment to their security, even if no reduction were made elsewhere. Such action certainly would strengthen doubts in Japan about America's willingness to remain involved anywhere in Asia. Although the MST, a substantial naval presence, and the nuclear guarantee still would provide reassurance to Tokyo, confidence regarding conventional protection even for Japan would diminish.[25]

CHANGES IN NUCLEAR STRATEGY. Some doubts about Washington's strategic nuclear commitment also have arisen in recent years, indicating a partial shift from Tokyo's negative reaction to the Gaullist arguments

23. The problem of American credibility also extends to the Japanese public as a whole. See Douglas H. Mendel, "Japan's Defense in the 1970's: The Public View," *Asian Survey*, vol. 10 (December 1970), p. 1061: 30 percent believing in U.S. credibility, 39 percent not believing, and 31 percent not knowing. Concern over the U.S. commitment is evident in the Japanese defense plans discussed in the *New York Times*, March 4, 1973.

24. U.S. monetary difficulties and unilateral actions toward China and in defense of the dollar reinforced this attitude. See Kuzuji Nagasu, "Japanese Economy in the Seventies," *Japan Quarterly*, vol. 19 (April–June 1972), pp. 140–41. Nagasu develops his justification for disengagement from the United States on the premise that American economic power and the credibility of its intentions already form an "international Ancien Regime."

25. Reflection of the interplay of Nixon's China policy and the economic shocks with this increased concern for security is evident in a discussion of these factors as the basis of a proposal to end the MST, demilitarize Okinawa, and establish diplomatic relations with North Korea, as well as with Peking and Hanoi, by Misao Obata, "A New Course for Japan," *Japan Quarterly*, vol. 19 (January–March 1972), pp. 19–27.

about American unreliability presented by General Pierre Gallois—a French advocate of national military autonomy—during the mid-1960s. Nuclear parity between the Soviet Union and the United States now adds credence, even among analysts and officials who are far from the JSP-JCP persuasion, to the French argument that the United States might not risk its own security to preserve Japan from nuclear threat. A subtle variation on this theme holds that a global nuclear umbrella does exist and is a salient characteristic of a U.S.-Soviet détente that is modest but growing; but that at the same time the reliability of the unilateral U.S. nuclear umbrella gradually is decreasing.[26] Other academic experts who believe that the United States still enjoys nuclear superiority state, however, that even this has become a mere shadow of the past advantage; they, too, conclude that parity will soon be the rule, in quality as well as quantity, and they project the possibility of a Soviet lead by the late 1970s.

In regard to the Soviet Union, some defense experts conclude that the United States would find it difficult to act after Japan had been hit. Given this feeling the value of the nuclear guarantee rests in a Soviet unwillingness to risk retaliation; a danger rests in a Soviet belief that the United States would not react if the USSR were to take swift action against Japan. Those defense experts who believe that a Soviet threat is unlikely, but that an American response is dubious, place less reliance on deterrence generally.[27] But they support retention of the mutual security treaty because it is a valuable political instrument for sustaining good relations between Washington and Tokyo. They also acknowledge some residual security value in that the United States might act in time (within a few weeks) to help defend Japan against a conventional or combined conventional and nuclear attack. Should deterrence fail, and should adequate help not come quickly, this type of analysis might lead Japan to an early strategic accommodation in preference to losses above 10 percent of the population or to another occupation.[28]

26. This argument is eloquently presented by Junnosuke Kishida in "Ideas on Disarmament," *Japan Quarterly*, vol. 19 (April–June 1972), pp. 148–53, in which he favors renewed efforts at arms control, with vigorous Japanese initiatives.

27. See, for example, Makoto Momoi, "Japan's Defense Policies in the 1970's," in J. A. A. Stockwin (ed.), *Japan and Australia in the Seventies* (Sydney: Angus and Robertson, 1972), p. 113.

28. See the extensive article on Japan's defense concepts, strategy, and tentative plans in the *New York Times*, March 4, 1973, in which many of these concepts are elaborated in some detail. See also the editorial note in *Survival*, vol. 15 (July–August 1973), p. 184.

Continued Japanese uncertainty about U.S. credibility will require repeated American reassurances in the future about the adequacy of its retaliatory force and about the firmness of its strategic commitment. This, of course, is ironic, since in an age of détente the need for deterrence should recede, especially when the Soviet Union is preoccupied increasingly with China.

OFFICIAL AND PUBLIC AMBIVALENCE. Japanese government officials often bemoan the limited public understanding of the extent to which issues of conventional and nuclear security are interdependent. For example, security experts long have argued that the U.S. forces in Japan constitute a valuable hostage ensuring a response to an attack at the nuclear as well as the conventional level.[29] Although defense experts both within and outside government now see the presence of the U.S. force as having essentially a political importance, especially as détente gains strength, they continue to believe in the importance of the hostage argument.[30] On the other hand, the general public has not subscribed heavily to the argument, primarily out of a lack of concern about a serious threat from abroad. Nor has this public generally demonstrated a strong desire for the presence of a substantial American military force to guarantee direct U.S. nuclear protection.

Nevertheless, a certain ambivalence is reflected in unfavorable comparisons made by Japanese defense analysts between their country and Europe concerning the reliability of—and, by inference, the need for—the American commitment. They often argue that cultural and historic factors, differences in distance, and Europe's greater strategic significance make the U.S. commitment to the Atlantic tie far more reliable.[31]

The informed Japanese public and some officials therefore appear insecure about the reality of an American response to either a conventional or nuclear threat. The problem may increase in intensity despite—or perhaps because of—the general reduction in cold war tensions and

29. Osamu Kaihara, formerly chief of the secretariat of the Cabinet National Defense Council, often has been identified with the hostage argument. He made a vigorous presentation of Japan's dependence on the strength of U.S. nuclear and conventional deterrence in discussing the severe limitations of Japan's Self-Defense Force in his "Real Character of the U.S.-Japan Security Treaty as Is Seen in the Fourth Defense Power Consolidation Plan," *Asia* (May 1972).

30. See, for example, the discussions in the Japanese press of home porting aircraft carriers at Yokosuka, in chapter 3, below.

31. See, for example, Study Committee on National Security Problems, "Outlook for the Problems of U.S. Military Bases in Japan" (Tokyo, December 28, 1970; processed), pp. 12–13.

may further complicate the resolution of such difficult issues as Japanese defense strength and deployment of U.S. forces in Japan.

But although many Japanese are insecure about continued American reliability, they are at the same time determined to move to some degree out of America's shadow, to exercise greater national initiative on the world scene.

Japan's Quest for Autonomy and Innovation in Foreign Affairs

In seeking autonomous, imaginative, and benign initiatives in foreign policy, Japanese of all political views reflect renewed nationalistic feeling and a desire for alternatives to dependence on the United States for national security. Proposed alternatives range from diminished emphasis on the military aspects of the security treaty combined with cautious improvement of relations with China and the USSR to replacement of the mutual security treaty with nonaggression treaties with the big powers and maintenance of an equal distance from all.

The impulse toward autonomy also is reflected in official actions to deemphasize U.S.-Japanese relations.[32] The cabinet of Premier Kakuei Tanaka adopted this orientation to some degree, and the feeling permeated the Liberal Democratic party and bureaucratic ranks.[33] Although almost all Japanese agree on the need to reduce dependence on the United States, there are a multitude of opinions about how far Japan should go in pursuit of independence and about the degree to which it should maintain an interdependent relation with the United States. Strong advocates of autonomy argue that Western Europe can remain close to the United States because its people and culture differ less from the American in feeling or thought than do Asians.

Autonomy and the Mutual Security Treaty

It could be argued that a truly separate role for Japan would so strain the American connection as to make the consequently attenuated mutual

32. L. Jerold Adams sees Japan's treaty activities as pointing toward a lessening of commitment toward the United States and Western Europe—without, however, moving sharply away from such an orientation: "Japanese Treaty Patterns," *Asian Survey*, vol. 12 (March 1972), pp. 256–57.

33. Gerald L. Curtis noted a strong anti-American current in LDP campaigning in 1969, as well as arguments by some of that party's candidates stressing the temporary nature of the Mutual Security Treaty: "The 1969 General Election in Japan," *Asian Survey*, vol. 10 (October 1970), p. 863.

security treaty unacceptable to Washington. Still, most journalists and scholars who are outside leftist ranks and advocate autonomy do not seek to terminate the MST but want to remove Japan from what they consider its complete subservience to American influence. One approach this group supports is modification of the treaty so as to minimize its security aspects, while stressing its importance in ensuring friendly political relations as a means for sustaining close economic ties.[34] Any ensuing security gap should then be filled by improving Japan's relations with China and the Soviet Union—proceeding, of course, on parallel but separate lines in view of the hostility between those two powers.[35] Many advocates of this approach feel that U.S. bases, as physical evidence of Japan's dependence, must be eliminated. Critics call this requirement merely a self-imposed condition, since a country can follow an autonomous policy even with U.S. bases, as Western Europe has demonstrated.

The Japanese also are reluctant to confront the burdens of a self-contained yet engaged foreign policy. They see the economic costs of acting as a major power and the vulnerability inherent in Japan's inadequate defense. Although many Japanese advocate and take pride in the concept of autonomous defense,[36] now extended to Okinawa, the nation cannot prevent Soviet air and naval harassment along its shores and surveillance of its home islands, let alone protect lines of communication or begin to field an adequate deterrent force.[37]

Thus, the Japanese desire for autonomy contains much ambivalence. In particular, the U.S. stress on equality and reciprocity implies autonomy with unpalatable connotations: Japanese support of the United

34. Fuji Kamiya, for example, argues that the treaty is no longer meaningful in a military sense but takes on new importance as a symbol of the political relation and basic common interest in preventing a major Pacific crisis: "Japanese-U.S. Relations and the Security Treaty: A Japanese Perspective," *Asian Survey*, vol. 12 (September 1972), p. 724.

35. One argument for separate nonaggression pacts with China and the USSR to supplement the mutual security treaty can be found in Shinkichi Etō, "Japan and America in Asia during the Seventies," *Japan Interpreter*, vol. 7 (Summer–Autumn 1972), pp. 248–49.

36. An important thrust toward security autonomy was given by the director of the Defense Agency, Yasuhiro Nakasone, in a statement of March 1970, "Five Principles of Autonomous Defense." He discussed them in the Diet on March 18: see *Japan Times*, March 19, 1970.

37. Hiroshi Shinohara, "National Defense," *Japan Quarterly*, vol. 18 (April–June 1971), p. 158, observed that the Defense Agency pushed for autonomy in the draft of its 1970 white paper, but that the Foreign Ministry successfully insisted that this thrust be deleted. Emphasis was placed instead on cooperation with the United States.

States and perhaps assumption of essential burdens that the United States will no longer bear.[38]

Prospective Alternatives in Diplomatic and Economic Relations

Because of this uncertainty, advocates of new departures often make general and tentative proposals in charting a new course without proposing too great a departure from the U.S. security and economic relations. The theme of improved relations with Peking and Moscow runs through all such proposals because it reinforces the trend toward détente, increases Japan's autonomy, and opens potential avenues not dependent on Western goodwill.[39]

Many official and academic experts, however, do not favor the nonaggression pacts with the communist powers suggested by some Japanese, because they deeply distrust Moscow and see no concrete benefits in a Peking accord. Yet they believe that by following the American path in improving relations with the communist powers but acting on its own, Tokyo could strengthen its relations with its powerful neighbors without harm to its American security connection. Increased trade and communications would form a constructive aspect of this security policy, one that, by generating a friendlier atmosphere, could provide a buffer to sustain the general détente through periods of tension.

Even this cautious approach recognizes that increased dealings with Peking and Moscow would complicate relations with Washington, especially when Japan knowingly acts against U.S. interests. The Tanaka-Nixon meeting in Honolulu in mid-1972 demonstrated that to a considerable degree Japan could follow an autonomous diplomatic course without encountering American opposition. Japan gave highest priority to sustaining its American security tie, and on that basis—rather than on an "equal-distance-from-all" approach—pursued a more active diplomacy toward the communist states. How effectively the allies will coop-

38. See Kamiya, "Japanese-U.S. Relations," p. 718, on the U.S. shift, in President Nixon's reports, from "partnership" (in 1970) to "relations of friendly competition" (in 1971) to the stress on "equality and reciprocity" (in 1972).

39. R. M. Collick is even doubtful that a cautious new diplomacy is possible given the domestic constraints of an inward-looking public and an electorally weakened LDP, to say nothing of the restraints imposed by its great power relations: see *World Today*, vol. 29 (February 1973), pp. 82–86. Donald C. Hellmann has argued that Japan generally behaves reactively in foreign affairs, largely because its decisionmaking process prevents bold leadership. See his *Japanese Foreign Policy and Domestic Politics* (University of California Press, 1969), chaps. 1 and 9.

erate in the future remains to be seen, especially under less favorable international circumstances.[40]

Japanese foreign policy experts also are seriously considering a responsible role for themselves in regional affairs and, more ambitious still, a larger world role, but one that avoids reliance on armaments.[41] Despite the uneasiness noted above, there is a sense of excitement in the informed public sector, if not in the government itself, about the idea of pioneering a new political endeavor, of becoming a major power without military force.

These objectives have much to commend them, but they still depend on a close relation with the United States. They also are subject to frustration—as in Asian suspicions of Japanese intentions or opposition to Japan's gaining a permanent seat on the UN Security Council. And balance-of-power politics remains a considerable factor in maintaining an equilibrium with Peking, however opportune the circumstances. Even a cautious and relatively altruistic regional economic policy will not diminish Peking's hostility, since political competition for regional influence is a critical ingredient of the Sino-Japanese rivalry.[42] Thus, the U.S. connection and its security component will remain important, even if

40. Both Kamiya, "Japanese-U.S. Relations," p. 723, and Johnson, "China and Japan," p. 720, see Taiwan as a critical issue in the future triangular relations of the United States, Japan, and China.

41. Herman Kahn and Max Singer see Japan as an emerging regional power of considerable proportions, already going beyond the limits of the Greater East Asia Co-Prosperity Sphere of the 1930s and early 1940s in terms of economic impact. They indicate that others had best treat Japan carefully lest Tokyo's wrath be aroused. See their "Japan and the Pacific Area in the 1970's," *Asian Survey,* vol. 11 (April 1971), pp. 406–12. Akira Ōnishi, however, sees Japan's record as one of putting its own production and other interests first and warns that it must change its course and help the Southeast Asians to develop if it is to avoid catastrophe: "Japan's Interest in Southeast Asia—A Japanese View," *Asian Survey,* vol. 11 (April 1973), pp. 413–21.

42. Collick sees scope for Japan as a regional power as a counterweight to China, but notes that fear of Tokyo's domination is a constraint throughout the region: *World Today,* p. 86. Similar concerns about Japan as a state to be feared are found in Makoto Yoshida, "How We Look to Southeast Asia," *Japan Quarterly,* vol. 18 (January–March 1971), pp. 32–39. Masataka Kōsaka notes that Japan cannot do much on a regional basis because its economic and security interests extend well beyond the area: "Japanese-American Relations in the Seventies," *Japan Interpreter,* vol. 7 (Winter 1971), p. 18. Donald C. Hellmann feels that the Sino-Japanese rivalry is bound to resume, in "The Confrontation with *Realpolitik*," in James W. Morley (ed.), *Forecast for Japan: Security in the 1970's* (Princeton University Press, 1972), pp. 161ff. Yamamuro holds the same view: "International Situation," p. 15.

camouflaged, as Japan moves into these new fields. If Japanese-American relations are to remain on an even course, the two powers still must confront and resolve bilateral security problems that trouble their relation.[43]

The Impact of Domestic Politics

From the beginning of the postwar period disagreement over foreign policy issues has been a major element in Japanese politics, the chief bone of contention being the security link with the United States. Controversy seems certain to continue and may be intensified as a result of social change in Japan and economic friction with the United States.

Security as a Partisan Issue

The Japanese public, as noted, gives little credence to the idea that the home islands face a threat from abroad, nor does it consider an American military presence essential to maintenance of the U.S. nuclear umbrella. The government, on the other hand, believes that the high degree of security currently enjoyed by Japan stems from the security tie and the American force presence. Furthermore, few Japanese express great concern about communist threats to other lands or regard these as jeopardizing their own security—with the possible exception of Korea. On all these issues, as well as on the need for a stronger defense establishment, a visible gap exists between the government and the public.

The even greater political distance between the Liberal Democratic party and the leftist opposition involves a complete disagreement over retaining the mutual security treaty and, in the case of the JSP, over the need for armed forces at all.[44] The JCP, adhering to a nationalist stance,

43. Should autonomy become identified with an anti-American course, the damage to bilateral relations could become severe. For a program advocating radical departures in foreign policy, including an end to the MST, no force in Okinawa, and stress on an anti-status quo but world-welfare approach, see Yoshikazu Sakamoto, "A New Foreign Policy," *Japan Quarterly*, vol. 19 (July–September 1972), pp. 270–80. For a nonmilitary, passive approach that sees China, although also a difficult power, as preferable to the United States or the Soviet Union, see Kyōzō Mori, "When the Cold War Ends," *Japan Quarterly*, vol. 18 (October–December 1971), pp. 392–401.

44. For a thorough review of left-wing party views from 1945 to 1964, see the entire issue of *JSPIJ*, vol. 3 (April 1965).

has adopted a more positive attitude toward national defense, but from a nonaligned posture. This position may seem more realistic and more internally consistent than that of the JSP, and, as the Japanese become increasingly nationalistic and reconciled to a substantial armed force, it could add to the JCP's appeal.[45] The public already favors the idea of autonomous defense for the nation, though not the force that it requires. Meanwhile, minority segments of the business community have advocated anti-American policies of economic nationalism, which amount to confrontation with the United States over issues of trade and investment. An extreme case was the attitude of the textile manufacturers in the last years of the Satō administration.[46] Should trade relations deteriorate, this belief could attract wider support within the business community.

Doubts and differences of opinion also affect the LDP because of its system of factional organization. Faction leaders, in maneuvering to strengthen their prospects for becoming premier, sometimes exploit popular distaste for aspects of the security relation with the United States, thus weakening the government's ability to defend the relationship. In the absence of a national consensus on foreign policy, especially defense-related matters, the government has proceeded slowly in developing new policies or even substantially modifying existing ones.

A related consequence has been the practice of conducting defense policy with a minimum of public discussion and heavy reliance on the accomplished fact, primarily to avoid additional political turmoil and to minimize the regime's identification with unpalatable security policies. This tactic reduces the effectiveness of the public forum as a means of educating the populace to the realities of international security considerations.

The opposition, of course, urges broader participation and the public

45. Kamiya emphasizes the JCP's nationalist posture: "Japanese-U.S. Relations," p. 720. For an earlier discussion of JCP relations with the major communist powers, see Paul Langer, *Communism in Japan* (Hoover Institute, 1972), chap. 5. John K. Emmerson discusses recent manifestations of independence, nationalism, and opposition to the great powers: "The Japanese Communist Party after Fifty Years," *Asian Survey*, vol. 12 (July 1972), pp. 573–76. On the socialists, see J. A. A. Stockwin, *The Japanese Socialist Party and Nationalism* (Melbourne University Press, 1968).

46. Kōsaka discusses the economic difficulties and takes the Japanese textile manufacturers to task for making unwarranted demands: "Japanese-American Relations," pp. 14–16 and 20–22. Another critic of the behavior of Japan's textile leaders is Genzō Hazama, "Behind the U.S.-Japan Textile War," *Japan Interpreter*, vol. 7 (Spring 1972), pp. 111–19.

airing of issues, hoping to compel a change of orientation.[47] Even supporters of the regime's policy emphasize the beneficial aspects of public
discussion.[48] Officials in particular note that the public has only a slight
grasp of the origins and purposes of the treaty and has never received a
clear and concise justification of the related base system. The public
is unaware, for example, that only Japan among America's Pacific allies
has no security obligation beyond areas under its administrative jurisdiction.[49]

Some officials argue that a clear exposition of basic defense policies,
an analytical evaluation of specific policy choices—for instance, armed or
unarmed neutrality—and a spirited justification of a streamlined base
structure provide the only means of obtaining the public support that is
so essential to maintain the existing security system. Such an approach
also could remove issues from the simple for-or-against context that now
colors policy debates.

Yet the fact remains that public justification of measures taken for
national defense has failed to evoke strong popular support, and the
LDP sees little value in a course that offers greater prospects for losing
than gaining votes.[50] Because politically the bases are the most vulnerable aspect of the security arrangements, even the pro-American Satō
regime adopted a "fewer-bases-the-better" approach rather than seeking

47. See, for example, Lawrence W. Beer, "Japan 1969: 'My Homeism' and
Political Struggle," *Asian Survey*, vol. 10 (January 1970), pp. 50–53.

48. They could point to the considerable support enjoyed by the government's
security policy at various times, as well as to the large number who were uncertain.
For example, in June 1969, when asked if Japan should give notice of a decision
to terminate the treaty in 1970, 24 percent of respondents replied yes, 32 percent
no, and 44 percent did not know. In September, 37 percent believed that the
treaty helped Japan as against 34 percent who replied in the negative. See Beer,
"Japan 1969," p. 52. In October 1969, a survey by NHK Television found 63
percent favoring maintaining or strengthening ties with the United States, as
against 13 percent who wanted them weakened. A poll on June 23, 1970, the
tenth anniversary of the MST, found 48 percent for the alliance (a rise of 8
percent over the previous poll), with 37 percent opposed: *Asahi Shimbun*, June
23, 1970. (The Williams College Roper Center holds a major collection of Japanese poll findings.)

49. Japan Institute of International Affairs (hereafter JIIA), *White Papers
of Japan 1970–71* (1972), p. 45.

50. The *Asahi* poll of June 23, 1970, for example, noted that a slim majority
favored abrogation of the treaty: 9 percent immediately and 42 percent eventually,
as against only 28 percent in favor of some continuation. (Interestingly enough,
37 percent believed the treaty to be beneficial, as against 14 percent who thought
otherwise.) By comparison, the *Jiji* press in October 1969 found that 48 percent

to justify any particular arrangement. Even those who have defended the MST system vigorously, as Prime Minister Tanaka did after taking office, carefully qualify their support by implying its maintenance for a modest length of time and promise frequent scrutiny to determine whether it still serves Japan's interests.

But this governmental timidity does not rest only on the simple if powerful consideration of electoral survival. This cautious approach enables a Japanese cabinet to use its critical opposition to press the United States for changes in arrangements, to resist U.S. proposals, or to delay a follow-through on agreements already reached. And by stepping aside it can deflect public wrath from itself to the United States and then adopt the role of mediator to minimize political damage to itself. Finally, the regime is not convinced that a direct, logical argument would necessarily carry the day.[51] It believes that, given its own uncertainties and the prevalence of conflicting views in the public realm, it is better to act as broker between the United States and the opposition than to have domestic political confrontation on clearly delineated issues.

Decentralization of power within Japan further complicates the government's task of controlling policy. In recent years prefectural and city governments, especially those in the hands of opposition parties, have been taking their own initiative on a broad range of issues, including those related to defense.[52] American bases and facilities are particularly vulnerable to real estate pressures, pollution controls, road and bridge

---

favored abrogation: 18 percent immediately and 30 percent eventually. Only 22 percent favored keeping the treaty as it is, whereas 15 percent wanted it changed from a military to a political alliance. For a recent discussion of public attitudes, see Wada Hideo, "Consciousness of Peace and National Security," in Hiroshi Itoh (ed.), *Japanese Politics: An Inside View* (Cornell University Press, 1973).

51. A most comprehensive series of studies on Japanese public opinion has been conducted by Douglas H. Mendel. For the earliest period, see his *The Japanese People and Foreign Policy* (University of California Press, 1961). His more recent surveys are "Japanese Views of Satō's Foreign Policy: The Credibility Gap," *Asian Survey*, vol. 7 (July 1967), pp. 444–56; "Japanese Opinions on Key Foreign Policy Issues," *Asian Survey*, vol. 9 (August 1969), pp. 625–39; and "Defense in the 1970's: The Public View," *Asian Survey*, vol. 10 (December 1970), pp. 1046–69. In the 1970 article, for example, 39 percent favored extension of the treaty beyond 1970, as against 19 percent opposed. But 42 percent responded "don't know." Moreover, the 39 percent fell to 14 percent when the question was asked about extending the treaty for at least a decade.

52. The incident in which the socialist mayor of Yokohama blocked a shipment of repaired tanks to Vietnam from the Sagami depot to the port captured national newspaper headlines for a few weeks in the summer of 1972.

regulations, and similar issues over which local needs, political ambitions, and policy differences often precipitate incidents.

Cultural and Economic Perspectives on Security

At the societal level, the growing diversity of occupational, age, and other interest groups also weakens the ability of the central government to control policy.[53] Business interests are becoming more diversified, and uniform support for a given governmental policy is less likely to be forthcoming. In addition, the postwar generation has a perspective on international affairs, on the American connection in particular, that is significantly different from that of its predecessor. Although prone to adopt American cultural norms, the younger generation favors greater independence from the United States, is quick to perceive government subservience to American dictates, and above all regards military vulnerability as less of a constraint on Japan's freedom to maneuver than does the older generation.

Japanese defense experts perceive the generation gap as directly relevant to their concern because of its philosophical overtones. The basic ideological orientation of freedom versus communism was persuasive to most Japanese after 1945. To the new generation, however, the distinction is devoid of meaning, unresponsive to the psychological and political problems the young consider significant. These Japanese analysts, including defense officials, recognize this as being a universal phenomenon, one that political leaders must strive to comprehend and accommodate.[54] How this will affect a new LDP leadership under electoral pressure is a central question.

Finally, Japan's economic growth adds another unsettling factor to

53. Masataka Kōsaka argues that the nonideological basis of the December 1972 election, which resulted in a sizable JCP gain, may be of significance because it could mark the beginning of a pragmatic bent on the part of voters, one directed at resolving particular problems. This in turn could make the framework of politics less rigid—but it also could hasten the end of the LDP majority, without its being replaced by its heterogeneous opposition. See his "Immobilism with a Future" (paper prepared for a conference of the Brookings Institution and the Japan Institute for International Affairs, January 1973; processed).

54. There is the further complication of a Japan growing more self-confident with regard to its own domestic achievements and yet still unsure of its image abroad. According to Yōnosuke Nagai, this places Japan in an "intermediate" political, economic, and cultural position and so generates an identity crisis: "Some Observations on the Perception Gap" (Tokyo Institute of Technology, 1972; processed).

the already unsteady course of its security policy. This growth and the consequent economic rivalry with the United States creates the risk—of much concern to Japanese economic analysts—that Washington will treat it as a scapegoat should the United States fail to solve its own structural difficulties. Japan in turn appears to American economic negotiators most stubborn in compromising on difficult issues.[55] It is quite possible, as one academic critic of Japan's present defense policy wryly observed, that economic differences will persist, and therefore Tokyo, to remain on good terms with the United States, will continue to make concessions in the security sector. A deterioration in economic ties, however, could lead to a worsening—or, less dramatically, to a thinning out —of relations in security and political matters. The Japanese business community could become more divided than ever on the value of close ties with the United States.

Potential for Redirecting the Relation

One remedial suggestion is for Japan and the United States to reduce their emphasis on the security nature of the treaty and to stress those clauses pertaining to political friendship and economic cooperation. Much can be said for such an approach: in sustaining bilateral friendship, in giving Tokyo a supporter in multilateral economic bargaining, and in keeping Japan aligned and without nuclear weapons. At the same time, the tie would still sustain the crucial guarantee against threat of attack and preserve the balance of major powers in Asia. Yet such an arrangement would end or sharply reduce Japan's security undertakings without a similar reduction of American burdens.

These arguments resemble in some degree those proposals of a decade ago for a deemphasized or skeletal MST, although in those instances the stress was on giving Japan a quasi-neutral status, as a guaranteed state without a security treaty.[56] In more recent years, other suggested revi-

55. Nagai refers often to the unsettling issues of economic discord, pointing up weaknesses that he notes among Japan's political and bureaucratic leaders, as well as the jingoist excesses of the press: "Social Attitudes and External Policy" (paper prepared for a conference on Social and External Factors Influencing Japanese Foreign Policies During the 1970s, held by the International Institute for Strategic Studies and the Japan Institute for International Affairs, 1972; processed).

56. Sakamoto, as cited in *JSPIJ*. In his 1959 article "A Defense Plan," Sakamoto advocated an end to the U.S.-Japanese treaty of 1952 and a Locarno type great-power arrangement to guarantee Japan's security.

sions also attempted to reduce Japan's military involvement and burden: by eliminating or sharply reducing U.S. base facilities, providing for the withdrawal of U.S. forces and their return only in an emergency, reducing the area of possible Japanese involvement by pulling back from the Korean and Taiwan commitments of 1969, and using the right of prior consultation to monitor and control U.S. military activity more closely.[57]

The specific issues apart, a reduction of Tokyo's obligation to such a low level probably would leave the accord with little meaning in American eyes, and both Foreign Ministry and defense officials are fully aware of that problem. Without mutuality, would even the nuclear guarantee retain its validity? Japanese officials also see danger in the call for formal revision of the accord on any of these matters, since it could lead to American counterproposals of a politically embarrassing nature.[58] They are acutely aware that reciprocity, taken literally, means an American right to call for the dissolution of the treaty, something the Japanese public does not consider since they view the MST as essentially a benefit to the United States and not to Japan. There is also a feeling among officials that the American government is unhappy over what it sees as unbalanced benefits weighted in Japan's favor and continuing inadequacies in Japan's implementation of treaty arrangements. A call for revision also would place the more basic issue of retaining the treaty squarely in the center of Japan's volatile domestic political arena.[59]

With the quest for change countered by such strong arguments about the risks involved, the Japanese government is most likely to follow a cautious middle path. It will seek concessions from the United States on specific operational issues while treading a difficult negotiating line: between, on the one hand, domestic pressures against the alliance, and, on the other, the needs and interests of its American ally.

57. Many of these points also were discussed earlier in Yōnosuke Nagai, "Japan's Foreign Policy Objective in a Nuclear Milieu," *JSPIJ*, vol. 5 (April 1967), pp. 27–43; and Kōsaka, "Japan as a Maritime Nation."

58. Although proposing a U.S. force withdrawal, the Study Committee on National Security Problems did not favor treaty revision, fearing the volatile nature of such a process in the current fluid international situation: "Outlook for the Problems of U.S. Military Bases in Japan" (Tokyo, December 28, 1970; processed), pp. 19–20.

59. In a speech on January 11, 1973, Foreign Minister Ohira firmly rejected proposals to revise the MST: *New York Times,* January 12, 1973.

CHAPTER THREE

THE MUTUAL SECURITY RELATION IN PRACTICE

In the more than twenty years of Japanese-American alliance, the security relation has been shaped and reshaped as the two governments handled the wide range of legal, diplomatic, military, and other practical questions that inevitably arose. Some were of major consequence. How much would the United States be able to use its Japanese bases to support combat activities and defense relations elsewhere in the Far East, in Korea, Vietnam, and Taiwan? How great a security interest would Japan express in these areas? What would be the size and shape of the U.S. troop presence on the Japanese islands and of the laws governing U.S. bases? How much prior consultation would be required before major changes were made in U.S. troop or weapons deployment? How much would U.S. military operations and plans be coordinated with those of Japan's Self-Defense Force?

The Mutual Security Treaty of 1960

The arrangement currently in force, the mutual security treaty of 1960, differs in several important respects from the original security pact of 1952, which has been aptly described by the Japanese as merely a troop-stationing accord that did not clearly obligate the United States to defend Japan.[1] The treaty of 1952 went somewhat against the grain of the Japanese constitution by proclaiming Japan's inherent right of self-defense, as well as its right to enter into collective security arrange-

1. The main Japanese complaints against the treaty of 1952 were summarized by Assistant Secretary of State J. Graham Parsons, in *Treaty of Mutual Cooperation and Security with Japan,* Hearings before the Senate Committee on Foreign Relations, 86 Cong. 2 sess. (1960), pp. 30–31. On the treaty of 1952, see Bernard C. Cohen, *The Political Process and Foreign Policy: The Making of the Japanese Peace Settlement* (Princeton University Press, 1957).

ments.[2] The United States, on its side, expressed its willingness to keep armed forces in Japan, but it expected Tokyo to increase its own defense efforts yet avoid armaments that "could be an offensive threat."[3] There were two unequal provisions: U.S. forces could be used, at Japan's request, to quell internal disturbances instigated from abroad; and Japan could not grant base rights to a third party without American approval. The treaty was to run indefinitely, with no restriction on American use of the bases or deployment of its forces from Japan.[4]

The Japanese had sought a security accord, having recognized early in the American occupation that they could be secure only with U.S. protection. For this, they were willing to pay the price of bases and facilities. Both parties agreed that Japan should not develop independent military power, but the United States, represented by John Foster Dulles, pressed for an establishment of 300,000 men under arms; the Japanese, wanting only a minimal commitment, grudgingly agreed to half that number. The two sides differed sharply also on the extent of Japan's security interests abroad, with the Americans pressing for greater concern and Japan, again successfully, restricting itself to the home islands.[5]

Provisions of the Treaty

The onerous clauses of the treaty of 1952—the lack of an overt American commitment and the absence of any Japanese obligation—led both sides to seek revision.[6] The mutual security treaty of 1960 com-

2. Article IX of the Japanese constitution states that "the Japanese people forever renounce war as a sovereign right of the nation and the threat or use of force as a means of settling international disputes.

"In order to accomplish the aim of the preceding paragraph, land, sea, and air forces, as well as other war potential, will never be maintained. The right of belligerency of the state will not be recognized." On the origins of the article, see Theodore McNelly, "The Renunciation of War in the Japanese Constitution," *Political Science Quarterly*, vol. 77 (September 1962), pp. 350–78.

3. John K. Emmerson, *Arms, Yen and Power: The Japanese Dilemma* (Dunellen, 1971), pp. 73–74.

4. Treaties and Other International Acts Series (hereafter TIAS) 2491, signed September 8, 1951, in force April 28, 1952. Parsons, *Treaty of Mutual Cooperation, Hearings*, pp. 30–31.

5. Emmerson, *Arms*, pp. 64–66. On the origins and development of Japanese security concepts in the post–World War II period, see also Martin Weinstein, *Japan's Postwar Defense Policy 1947–1968* (Columbia University Press, 1971).

6. On the problems and negotiations in the late 1950s, see Fred Greene, *U.S. Policy and the Security of Asia* (McGraw-Hill, 1968), pp. 87–91.

mitted the United States specifically to the defense of Japan but obliged Japan to defend only the territories under its jurisdiction. This meant at the time the four home islands and by implication included the U.S. bases and facilities stationed there, but excluded Okinawa and other islands of the Ryukyu chain, then under U.S. jurisdiction. Japan, unlike other Pacific area signatories of treaties with the United States, undertook no obligation to act if U.S. territory were attacked or in defense of U.S. interests at sea. On the other hand, the United States retained rights to its bases and facilities, not only for the defense of Japan but also for international peace and security in the Far East.

The two derogations on Japan's sovereignty were eliminated and Japan and the United States were obliged to act to meet a common danger only in accord with their individual constitutional provisions and processes. At American insistence, to assure periodic review, the treaty was to run for ten years, with each party having the right of abrogation thereafter with one year's notice.[7] Finally, under an Eisenhower-Kishi exchange of notes, the United States assured Japan that it would engage in prior consultation before undertaking a major deployment of American forces to Japan, making a major change in combat equipment in Japan, or using Japanese bases for combat operations to be undertaken elsewhere.[8]

The Japanese have observed that the title of the new treaty stresses mutuality: it was a "treaty of mutual cooperation and security" between Japan and the United States, whereas the 1951 accord had been simply a "treaty of security." Not only is it a joint defense treaty instead of a facilities-providing accord, but also it calls for political and economic cooperation. Article II provides that the signatories contribute to peaceful and friendly international relations, seek elimination of conflict in economic policies, and encourage economic collaboration.[9] Although universally considered a security alliance, it contains the basis for broader interaction between the two countries. This point may become

7. TIAS 4509, signed January 19, 1960, in force June 23, 1970; Secretary of State Christian A. Herter, in *Treaty of Mutual Cooperation,* Hearings, pp. 3–6; Greene, *U.S. Policy,* pp. 91–92; Emmerson, *Arms,* pp. 80–88.

8. For texts, see *United States Security Agreements and Commitments Abroad: Japan and Okinawa,* Hearings before the Subcommittee on U.S. Security Agreements and Commitments Abroad of the Senate Committee on Foreign Relations, 91 Cong. 2 sess. (January 26–29, 1970), pt. 5, pp. 1435–38 (referred to hereafter as Hearings).

9. Takuya Kubo, "Revaluation of Japan-U.S. Security Treaty," written in April 1972 for the June 1972 issue of *Kokubō,* p. 1.

more significant should efforts gain ground to reduce the military emphasis of this relation.

CLARIFICATION OF MUTUAL RESPONSIBILITIES. With the emergence of China as a nuclear power in 1964, the Japanese sought further assurance of American protection against a strategic threat from Peking. On November 18, 1964, the Security Research Council of the Liberal Democratic party (LDP) recommended a stronger security program and a reaffirmation of the MST.[10] This led to the Johnson-Satō communiqué of January 13, 1965, which stated that "the President reaffirms the United States' determination to abide by its commitment under the treaty to defend Japan against any armed attack from the outside." Although the wording was somewhat elliptical, the word "any" was meant to cover the new Chinese problem. The language actually seemed stronger than that of the treaty, which called on both "to act to meet the common danger." Deputy Undersecretary of State U. Alexis Johnson held that no real change had been made, and emphasized that the MST for the first time obligated Japan as well as the United States to contribute to Japan's defense. He observed that only if Japan made such an effort would the United States remain committed.[11] Technically, then, the Johnson-Satō communiqué did not constitute an additional U.S. undertaking, but politically the United States was reaffirming its obligation to act in any instance in which Japan, given its limited military capacity, would be unable to defend itself. Japan's first defense white paper, issued on October 20, 1970, reiterated this obligation and referred also to the statement by Secretary of Defense Melvin Laird to Japan Defense Agency Director Nakasone on September 14, 1970, which confirmed the readiness of the United States to "use all types of weapons for the defense of Japan."[12]

In the Satō-Nixon communiqué of 1969, the United States agreed to the reversion of Okinawa. According to that document and the accompanying speech by Satō on November 21, 1969, Japan in turn extended its own obligations to a degree. The communiqué marked the first formal

10. Kei Wakaizumi, "Chinese Nuclear Armament and the Security of Japan," *JSPIJ*, vol. 4 (December 1966).

11. Hearings, pp. 1188–89.

12. Japan Defense Agency, "The Defense of Japan" (October 1970; processed), p. 21. See also Emmerson, *Arms*, p. 82; and Makoto Momoi, "Japan's Defense Policies in the 1970's," in J. A. A. Stockwin (ed.), *Japan and Australia in the Seventies* (Sydney: Angus and Robertson, 1972), p. 104, in which Momoi states that Secretary Laird made this promise to Nakasone in September 1970.

reaffirmation of interest by both parties in continuing the MST indefinitely.[13] In addition, it restricted American use of bases on Okinawa—following actual reversion in 1972—to the terms applicable to the home islands; but by extending Japanese jurisdiction to the Ryukyus, it made Japan responsible for the defense of that area and of the U.S. facilities there against a conventional attack.[14]

Most important, Japan for the first time officially recognized that the security of Japan was related to the peace and security of the Far East, as well as to the U.S. ability to carry out its obligations to other states in the area.[15] This was noted both in the communiqué and in the Satō speech, which stated that it was "impossible adequately to maintain the security of Japan without international peace and security in the Far East." Satō added that the Japanese response during prior consultations about deployment of U.S. forces from Japan for combat abroad would have to be determined in that light. He noted that South Korea was essential to Japan's security, and thus Tokyo's policy would be to decide "promptly and positively" about U.S. use of Japanese bases for military combat operations to meet an armed attack against Seoul.

Satō was more circumspect regarding Taiwan: he neither described its security as an essential Japanese interest nor committed Japan to a favorable response under prior consultation. Still, he recognized that if the United States had to invoke its treaty commitment to the Republic of China (ROC), any situation requiring such action would constitute a threat to the peace and security of the Far East, including Japan.[16]

Taiwan was to reemerge as a potentially difficult issue when in 1972 Japan moved toward normalization of relations with China. But in part because Peking was anxious for moderate terms—assuring itself only of Japan's obligation to sever relations with the ROC and not to support an independent entity on Taiwan—the security aspects caused no difficulty at that time. The Nixon-Tanaka meeting in Honolulu on August 31 and September 1, 1972, led the Japanese to reaffirm that in their dealings with Peking they would not undermine any American security obliga-

13. Hearings, p. 1441.
14. Ibid., pp. 1167, 1441.
15. Ibid., pp. 1162–63.
16. Background given by Under Secretary of State U. Alexis Johnson, November 21, 1969, in Hearings, pp. 1439–44. The Hearings also contain the text of the Satō-Nixon communiqué (pp. 1425–28), and the Satō speech to the National Press Club in Washington, which was delivered during his visit and considered an integral part of the agreement (pp. 1428–33).

tions to Taiwan.[17] And during the Tanaka visit to China in September, the Chinese pressed neither the Taiwan security issue nor the MST itself.[18] This particular circle was closed in the Japanese legislature by reference to an understanding, first reached implicitly in the U.S.-Chinese Shanghai communiqué of February 1972, that Peking would not use force to reunite Taiwan with the mainland. Thus, the entire question of U.S.-Japanese security relations becoming entangled in a Taiwan-mainland confrontation was a hypothetical and nonoperational problem—as the relieved Japanese leadership constantly reiterated.[19]

PRINCIPAL UNDERSTANDINGS AND BENEFITS. The main features of this treaty system, then, are:

—A U.S. obligation to defend Japan

—A Japanese commitment to build a moderate-size, conventional defense establishment and to defend territories under its jurisdiction

—U.S. facilities in Japan to be used to support American commitments throughout East Asia

—Prior consultation before deployment of U.S. troops to combat outside Japan

—A Japanese undertaking to support U.S. security efforts in Korea, with the thorny Taiwan problem placed at least temporarily on the back burner

—Prior consultation before major deployments of U.S. forces to Japan or major changes in U.S. combat equipment—including the installation of nuclear weapons—in Japan

17. *New York Times,* September 2, 1972, carried the text of the communiqué. The omission of any reference to Taiwan in the communiqué was noted by the press. This clearly indicated a downgrading since 1969, but also it reflected Tokyo's willingness not to allow the issue to become a problem for U.S. defense obligations to the Republic of China in the course of improving Japan's relations with Peking. Prime Minister Tanaka noted the President's special concern about the stability of the ROC in the wake of Japan's improved relations with Peking: *New York Times,* September 3, 1972.

18. The Japanese informed the United States that the issue of the MST was never raised by the Chinese. *New York Times,* October 3, 1972. For the text of the Chinese-Japanese communiqué, see *New York Times,* September 30, 1972.

19. Foreign Minister Ohira spoke in this vein in the Diet, November 8, 1972. He also observed in the same forum on November 10, 1972, that the MST had not inhibited Japan from improving its relations with Moscow or Peking. The language in the U.S.-Chinese communiqué regarding Taiwan—text in the *New York Times,* February 28, 1972—was elliptical, but the "no force" understanding is spelled out in follow-up articles by Max Frankel, *New York Times,* February 29 and March 2, 1972.

The basic arrangement—though not all aspects, particularly the base questions and Japanese noninvolvement abroad—has been defended vigorously over the years as being in the best interests of both signatories. For the United States, it helped keep Japan out of communist control at a time of genuine fear of outside aggression and internal subversion. It serves now to avert a possible Japanese alignment with a major communist power and gives the United States some assurance against the revival of a fully armed, independent, and nationalist Japan. In particular, and especially during the 1960s, the United States saw Japan as an effective counterweight to China, the more valuable because it posed no military threat to its neighbors. And, as the treaty noted, the tie puts pressure on both parties to maintain friendly relations and provides a helpful setting for resolving difficult bilateral problems in other fields.[20]

Japan has received benefits as well from this last point, especially since the flare-up of economic antagonism in recent years. It has similar interests in a stable balance of power in Northeast Asia and in close relations with the remainder of the industrial world. Japan remains exposed to two major communist powers that have repeatedly expressed a serious desire to see its entire social structure overturned.[21] Despite the currently moderated intentions of these regimes, their capacity to exert pressure remains high. And the experience of the Soviet attack in 1945, in violation of the Japanese-Soviet neutrality treaty, serves as a reminder that when state interests clash, policies may change dramatically at the expense of a vulnerable state. Moreover, the American accord enables Japan not only to deny itself nuclear weapons but also to follow a more modest defense buildup in conventional forces than otherwise might be required.[22]

20. The advantage of the treaty and the value of the Japanese tie to the United States are discussed by Under Secretary Johnson in Hearings, p. 1216; and by Kubo, "Revaluation," p. 4–6.

21. Etsuo Kohtani, "Prospects for Power Relations in Asia and the Pacific" (July 1972; processed), pp. 10–11; and Kubo, "Revaluation," pp. 6–8.

22. Japan's reliance on the U.S. nuclear deterrent and its freedom to pursue limited defense objectives with a modest force are stated in a National Defense Council staff paper, "The Essence of Japan's Defense Power and a Program for Defense Equipment" (October 1966; processed), summarized in Martin E. Weinstein, "Defense Policy and the Self-Defense Forces," *Japan Interpreter*, vol. 6 (Summer 1970), p. 170.

Application of the Mutual Security Treaty Abroad

The treaty of 1960 expressed the common concern of both parties for the peace and security of the Far East and provided for consultation in case of threats to the peace and security of the area. Article VI, known as the "Far East clause," gave the United States base facilities in Japan as a means of assuring not only Japan's security but also "international peace and security in the Far East." Shortly after signing the treaty in January 1960, Japan defined the Far East as the area north of the Philippines, in and around Japan, the territory of the Republic of China and the Republic of Korea, the offshore Chinese islands of Quemoy and Matsu, Takeshima island, and the Soviet-occupied islands just north of Hokkaido—Shikotan, Habomai, Kunashiri, and Etorofu—that are claimed by Japan. After preliminary inclusion, Soviet and mainland Chinese territories were excluded.

The government remained vague on other details, and the idea of indirect Japanese involvement elsewhere in the Far East remained uncertain and controversial. Thus, in 1965 the Satō government said that the United States could use its bases in Japan—short of flying planes directly into combat—for the Vietnam war because this conflict posed a threat to peace and security in the Far East, even though Vietnam was excluded from the 1960 interpretation of the Far East.[23] This intensified criticism of the Far East clause, which now threatened to enmesh Japan in America's Asian conflicts.

Despite a poll in June 1969 that placed greatest popular dissatisfaction on the Far East clause,[24] the Satō visit to Washington that November underlined the importance of peace and security in the Far East—especially that of South Korea—to the security of Japan. This provided the rationale for Satō's favorable attitude toward the deployment of U.S. forces from Japan in case of aggression against the Republic of Korea (ROK).[25] In addition, "the maintenance of peace and security in the Taiwan area was also [an] important factor for the security of Japan." The less urgent and more ambiguous language reflected the lower secu-

23. A good discussion of this can be found in Emmerson, *Arms*, pp. 82–85.
24. *Yomiuri Shimbun*, August 1969.
25. Backgrounder briefing given by Under Secretary Johnson, November 21, 1969, in Hearings, pp. 1439–40.

rity priority and greater political delicacy of Taiwan, as compared with South Korea.[26] The Japanese therefore insisted on this distinction, despite U.S. efforts to have the wording identical to that applied to Korea.

This emergence from Japan's security shell had no immediate repercussions because the prime minister could point triumphantly to the long-sought return of Okinawa to Japanese jurisdiction—with no nuclear weapons. The United States recognized the lack of consensus behind this extension of Japan's security responsibility, but held that most Japanese would be disturbed by communist takeovers in Korea and Taiwan.[27] The judgment that Satō's position lacked popular support was valid, and opposition to any extraterritorial involvement in security problems was reasserted once the reversion of Okinawa was assured.

Antagonism in Japan to involvement in the security problems of others focused on the U.S. system of bases in Japan, since the Japanese constitution, public opposition to any interventions abroad by the Self-Defense Force (SDF), and the military limitations of the SDF make direct Japanese participation altogether unlikely. Tolerating the MST and a U.S. force presence only to protect Japan from a strategic threat, most Japanese oppose use of the bases for purposes unrelated to this single requirement, narrowly interpreted. A majority of the public views all other uses as serving only the interests of U.S. power politics in Asia and therefore opposes U.S. use of bases in Japan even to protect South Korea.[28]

More sophisticated and more recent Japanese concern centers on an interpretation of the Nixon doctrine that assigns Japan a heavier security burden in Asia while the United States reduces tensions with Peking. Not only would this impose heavier and foreign-related defense costs on Tokyo, but also Japan would become the focus of Chinese antagonism and thus risk its exclusion from the tension-reducing process. From the perspective of 1972–73, some scholars faulted Satō's 1969 trade-off for accepting a more exposed role in Asian security affairs, especially as the United States was preparing for détente with Peking. In fact, they argued

26. Under Secretary Johnson acknowledged "that the status of Korea is a much more direct and vital interest to Japan": ibid., p. 1191.

27. Ibid., p. 1419.

28. When asked to give the "most important reason" for the bases, 13 percent said they were to protect Japan; 12 percent, to protect other Asian countries; 44 percent, to protect the United States; 8 percent, all three equally; and 23 percent, do not know. *Jiji* press, September 1969.

that the Satō-Nixon communiqué provided one such foundation, greater indigenous Asian efforts while the United States reduced its presence, for the eventual Sino-American rapprochement—a point that Satō failed to grasp in his fixed concern over reversion of Okinawa.[29]

Korea

Given this orientation, the Shanghai communiqué of February 1972 reinforced Japanese determination not to assume a heavier security burden in Asia. In particular, they did not want to be pushed into defending South Korea. Under no circumstances did they want a reduced U.S. military presence there if it meant that Japan was to pick up the slack.

KOREA AND JAPANESE SECURITY. But was South Korea's security a vital interest to Japan? Clearly the divergent attitudes expressed in 1969 between the public and the policymakers revealed a serious gap. Security planners were concerned over the internal threat that communist aggression on the peninsula would pose to the home islands.[30] Those who fashioned the 1969 communiqué believed that all Japanese, including the opposition in private, agreed that Japan had a stake in the security of South Korea. They argued that the indication of concern expressed in the communiqué was proper and acceptable, as reflected by the absence of complaints during the following years. They defended the distinction between Korea and Taiwan—a prudent one in retrospect— and noted that the issue in any event is not Japanese involvement but

29. This was all the more disturbing because of Peking's and Pyongyang's vigorous propaganda campaign against Japan that extended from 1970 into the early months of 1972, when it began slacking off preparatory to the Sino-Japanese settlement of September 1972. At the height of the campaign, the communist regimes accused Tokyo of planning a reversion to militarism, expansion, and domination over Southeast Asia and of acting as a replacement for the fading American "imperialists." A summary view of alleged Chinese proofs of Japanese militarism was given by Hiroshi Shinohara, "National Defense," *Japan Quarterly*, vol. 18 (April–June 1971), pp. 159–60. A vigorous Japanese counterargument to the Chinese position is in Hidejirō Kotani, "Views on the Resurgence of Militarism," *Japan Interpreter*, vol. 8 (Spring 1973), pp. 196–201.

30. Matsueda Tsukasa and George E. Moore, "Japan's Shifting Attitude toward the Military: *Mitsuya Kenkyū* and the Self-Defense Force," *Asian Survey*, vol. 7 (September 1967), pp. 614–25; and Weinstein, *Japan's Postwar Defense Policy*.

support of American resistance to aggression.[31] Some defense experts have, in fact, criticized the Satō undertaking of 1969 as a meaningless commitment that demonstrated U.S.-Japanese friendship as well as Tokyo's desire to do something in an emergency, but did not obligate Japan to any specific undertaking.

The truth lies somewhere in the middle. Satō did commit Japan to an offer of base facilities and a friendly political attitude, but without its own direct involvement in the event that the United States defended Seoul against aggression. Even this modest undertaking could be controversial in light of potential public opposition, though American use of bases might be acceptable, in contrast to their use in the Vietnam war. Seoul's fear that reversion of Okinawa would reduce the U.S. capability to defend the peninsula also lay behind Japan's more positive position in 1969.[32] The communiqué then became a reassurance, to both Washington and Seoul, that the United States would receive from Japan cooperation similar to that enjoyed during the Korean war.

Japanese foreign affairs and defense officials agree on the importance of South Korea's security to Japan and recognize that American bases in Japan directly support this objective. They also consider a U.S. force presence in Korea important to the security of Japan and of Asia as a whole. The political opposition, however, denies the validity of a Japanese interest in the security of Korea or at best holds that a reduction of tension there—with no military backing to Seoul—is the only sensible way to resolve this problem.[33] Some foreign affairs analysts be-

---

31. See also Masataka Kōsaka, "Options for Japan's Foreign Policy," *Adelphi Papers,* no. 97 (London: International Institute for Strategic Studies, 1973), pp. 7–8. In his opening statement before the Senate subcommittee, Under Secretary Johnson observed that the Japanese authorities believed "that the biggest threat to Japanese security lies in the continual tension on the Korean peninsula. While the North Koreans cannot directly threaten Japan, a communist take-over of the entire peninsula would seriously affect Japan's security interests, and a Korean conflict, with all the uncertainties it would unloose of possible participation by the major powers, would clearly affect Japan's own security": Hearings, p. 1418.

32. This concern was noted by the Study Committee on National Security Problems in "Outlook for the Problems of U.S. Military Bases in Japan" (Tokyo, December 28, 1970; processed), p. 21.

33. See, for example, Takashi Saitō, "Japan and Korean Unification," *Japan Interpreter,* vol. 8 (Winter 1973), pp. 33–36. He strongly denounces South Korea as a militant state, takes a friendly stand toward the North, and calls for unification. Both Saitō and Obata Misao ("A New Course for Japan," *Japan Quarterly,* vol. 19 [January–March 1972], pp. 19–27) call for the recognition of North Korea.

lieve that, as long as the MST exists, the public would not be upset by an American troop withdrawal from Korea; others note that most Japanese view the Korean Strait as a protective hazard and scarcely are concerned about the presence or absence of U.S. troops on the peninsula.

U.S. PRESENCE ON THE PENINSULA. Thus, a gap exists between the government and the public regarding the importance of a U.S. military presence in Korea, as well as on the question of whether the security of Korea is a vital Japanese interest.[34] In contrast to the indifference of the public, defense experts and officials value the security benefits of a continued U.S. security commitment to Korea; they are especially anxious that a new wave of isolationism in the United States not revive the concept of 1949–50, which placed the peninsula beyond the U.S. zone of defense. Japanese defense officials expected U.S. troop withdrawals from the peninsula under the Nixon doctrine, but they fear that a complete withdrawal would lead to the end of the U.S. defense commitment in Korea. They would find tolerable the withdrawal of all ground combat forces, provided U.S. Air Force and other elements remained there. But they would view a total removal of American forces from Korea, even with a U.S. military position remaining in Japan, as a sign of deterioration in U.S.-Japanese relations and a portent of a withdrawal from Japan itself, a circumstance bringing the MST into question.

There are, however, differences of opinion among the Japanese academic experts about the effect of the withdrawal of U.S. forces from either Japan or Korea, provided combat elements remained in one of these countries. Some, stressing the evident popular repugnance toward a force and base presence in Japan, believe that a concentration of U.S. forces in Korea would be the more acceptable alternative. Others feel that such a move would constitute an American abandonment of Japan, even though the U.S. forces in Korea actually protected the home islands.

---

34. Kunio Muraoka argued against a cooperative attitude toward the U.S. use of Japanese bases to defend South Korea, since there would be no national consensus for such involvement: "Japanese Security and the United States," *Adelphi Papers*, no. 95 (London: International Institute for Strategic Studies, 1973), p. 22. Kim Sam-kyu, a Korean writing for a Japanese audience, argued that South Korea was vulnerable and that Korean security was of considerable importance to Japan; he saw peaceful unification as the key, but without advocating how this was to be achieved or what form of government would emerge: "The Korean Question," *Japan Quarterly*, vol. 17 (January–March 1970), pp. 37–44.

Thus, opinion is mixed on the value to Japan of a continued U.S. troop presence in Korea. Though many observers probably would react uneasily to a complete American withdrawal from the peninsula, the fact that an American presence in Korea protects Japan does not strengthen public sentiment in favor of U.S. bases in Japan, though the facilities sustain such a mainland deployment. In fact, there is widespread popular unwillingness to permit the use of U.S. bases in Japan to defend Korea, despite the government's 1969 undertaking; and it goes without saying that Japan would not become directly involved in a military effort to defend Korea.[35] Since tensions on the peninsula have diminished, this has not been an active political issue, especially with Taiwan occupying the spotlight. Should a threat to South Korea again materialize, however, an acute clash could develop over Japanese policy.[36]

For the present, the opposition will be more likely to advocate abrogation of the 1969 commitment on the grounds that the danger has passed. A genuine move toward stability in Korea actually could include a gradual reduction of U.S. forces without raising alarms in Seoul or Tokyo. In such a situation, a residual American presence on the peninsula would assure Japan against a repetition of 1950, and it could be justified publicly as contributing to the relaxation of tensions rather than as a source of danger. Under these conditions the 1969 undertaking could probably survive opposition challenges, though primarily by evading the central issue and pointing out that it will not require implementation in the near future.[37]

35. A February 1970 public opinion poll indicated that although 27 percent favored increased Japanese responsibility for security and defense of the Far East, as against 28 percent opposed and 45 percent "do not know," only 7 percent responded affirmatively when asked if Japan should send the SDF to defend South Korea in the event of an attack from the North: Douglas H. Mendel, "Japan's Defense in the 1970's: The Public View," in *Asian Survey*, vol. 10 (December 1970), pp. 1055–57.

36. Cho Soon Sung observed that Japan did not take a sympathetic interest in Korean questions. Even those who did, he pointed out, still wished to stay clear of commitments, and in fact considered the 1965 treaty establishing diplomatic relations between Japan and the Republic of Korea as too much of an obligation even though it contained no security undertakings: "Japan's Two Koreas Policy and the Problem of Korean Unification," *Asian Survey*, vol. 7 (October 1967), pp. 703–25. For a blow-by-blow description of the parliamentary struggle for ratification of the 1965 treaty, see Hans W. Baerwald, "The Diet and the Japan-Korea Treaty," *Asian Survey,* vol. 8 (December 1968), pp. 951–59.

37. This in effect extends to Korea the Tanaka-Ohira line of reasoning about the danger of becoming involved in Taiwan: that is, that the communists will see to it that the issue does not arise.

MULTILATERAL GUARANTEES OF KOREAN STABILITY. Many Japanese scholars feel that a four-power guarantee of the Korean peninsula by means of a nonaggression pact would facilitate détente between the two Koreas. But détente on the peninsula worries some Japanese experts on Korea in one important respect: they fear that a unified peninsula, regardless of how achieved or under whose rule, would create tension between Korea and Japan. Mutual antagonisms fueled by specific irritants such as treatment of minorities or fishing rights could lead to a dangerous confrontation. There is a latent fear that a war could arise between Japan and Korea in the next generation if the Koreans did unite, since unification would remove North-South antagonisms and point all energies toward such a confrontation. The experts therefore conclude that Japan's security is best served by a divided Korea that accepts the status quo and with it reduced tension in the area—somewhat along the lines of the agreement between East and West Germany.

Japan, however, could not undertake military operations to sustain a détente agreement against violation by an aggressor. Rather, the purpose of such a pact would be to get a commitment from Moscow and Peking—along with the United States and Japan—not to support aggression and so in effect to deter Pyongyang from contemplating such a course. Japanese Foreign Ministry officials, particularly those concerned about the durability of American security commitments in Asia, see danger in a multilateral treaty approach, since it could end the U.S.-South Korean treaty and set a precedent for eroding the MST.

KOREA AND U.S.-JAPANESE RELATIONS. To some Japanese defense experts, private and official, Tokyo's position on Korea is so limited that it contributes to the instability in U.S.-Japanese security relations. By defending South Korea and maintaining a force there, the United States pays a considerable cost, increases Japan's security, and widens Tokyo's freedom of diplomatic action. The inequality of burden eventually may make it unacceptable to the American public, which then might demand an end to the undertaking or insist that Japan carry a greater share of the load. Such pressure, however, could jeopardize even the limited Japanese undertakings of the 1969 accord, which have escaped major challenge because of the remote likelihood of their becoming operational. Thus, a combination of increased tension on the peninsula, a significant reduction of the American position in Asia, and an effort by the United States to force greater Japanese responsibility in the peninsula could place Korea in the foreground of problems affecting U.S.-Japanese security relations.

Taiwan

The issues concerning Taiwan differ markedly in several respects from those concerning Korea. The area is less vital to Japan, but it represents a sensitive issue in relations with Peking and became a live political problem in the wake of Sino-American détente. The Shanghai communiqué of 1972 in effect underwrote the island's status quo for the immediate future by failing to question the U.S.-ROC defense treaty or to require a change in diplomatic relations between Washington and Taipei as a price for détente.[38] The United States, however, promised to reduce and eventually withdraw all forces from Taiwan and undertook in effect not to support the establishment of an independent state there in the future. For its part, Peking not only accepted the security status quo but also tacitly agreed not to use force to take over Taiwan.[39] This removed the security issue from Sino-Japanese negotiations and assured Chinese abstinence from attacks on the MST and its linkage to Taiwan.

JAPANESE STANCE. Japan paid only a political price for normalization in September 1972: by declaring its 1952 peace treaty with the Republic of China no longer in effect, by severing diplomatic ties with Taipei, and by stating that it "understands and respects" the claim of the People's Republic of China that China and Taiwan are one. And just as the United States protected its vital interest, the security of Taiwan against acts of force, so Japan sustained its major interest, significant economic contacts with Taiwan.[40]

The new Tanaka cabinet therefore was able to reassure the United States it would not complicate Washington's commitment to the ROC by raising questions about American use of facilities in Japan to main-

---

38. For a transcript of Secretary Kissinger's news conference in Shanghai and the text of the Shanghai communiqué, see *New York Times,* February 28, 1972.

39. For a description of this trade-off and other aspects of the bargaining, see Max Frankel, "Whole China Communique Was Intensely Negotiated," *New York Times,* March 2, 1972.

40. Richard Halloran, "Tanaka Cautious on Chinese Ties," *New York Times,* October 1, 1972. In a poll in November 1966, for example, among those favoring recognition of Peking, 76 percent favored continuing relations with Taipei, 6 percent wanted to cancel relations, and 18 percent did not know: Douglas H. Mendel, "Japanese Opinions on Key Foreign Policy Issues," *Asian Survey,* vol. 9 (August 1969), p. 634. Lawrence Olson describes the majority of Japanese as wanting official relations with Peking but at a loss about how to solve the Taiwan problem and therefore going along with the government's wait-and-see policy: *Japan in Postwar Asia* (Praeger, 1970), p. 101.

tain peace and security in the Far East, including Taiwan. At the Honolulu meeting and later, Prime Minister Tanaka reaffirmed that the Taiwan region remained part of the Far East to which the MST applies. He also stated before the Diet that normalization of relations with China did not involve the MST, that the Far East clause remained valid, and that there was no need to renounce the 1969 communiqué.[41] Similarly, Foreign Minister Ohira presented the cabinet's unified view, reaffirming Taiwan's inclusion in the treaty's Far East clause and keeping open the option of American use of the bases should a conflict arise. In dealing with the question of what Japan actually would do in the event of a conflict in the Taiwan Strait area, the government stated that this was not just a hypothetical question but one that could not possibly arise since the Peking regime had committed itself not to use force.[42]

Nonetheless, this stand was a tenuous one, even with a moderate attitude in Peking, and the opposition attacked hard where the government is vulnerable. It warned of possible Japanese involvement through the MST in U.S. efforts to preserve Taiwan against a mainland attack, even though Tokyo in effect had recognized the Taiwan problem as an internal Chinese affair. The Sino-Japanese communiqué, however, did not explicitly recognize Taiwan as Chinese territory, and the government avoided a clarification for fear of the political difficulties involved.[43] In fact, it was moving toward such recognition, thus increasing its vulnerability, since the Tanaka cabinet's unified view also acknowledged that Taiwan was a "Chinese internal affair." This strengthens the opposition's argument that a future PRC-ROC confrontation would be a civil war in which Japan should not become involved. Finally, the unified view referred to "future friendly relations between Japan and China," indicating further that Japan earnestly seeks to avoid any involvement in possible hostilities in the Taiwan Strait.[44] Even more than in the case of Korea, it relies on peaceful communist policies to avoid a potentially grave divergence between the United States and Japan.

POTENTIAL EFFECT ON U.S.-JAPANESE RELATIONS. A favorable situation actually may develop in which the United States remains committed to the island's defense, Peking adheres to a policy of no force, and Taiwan continues to thrive economically, with substantial links to

41. Statements in the Diet, November 2, 1972.
42. In the Diet, November 8, 1972.
43. Questions and answers in the Diet, November 2, 1972.
44. Ohira position in the Diet, November 8, 1972.

Japan.[45] Even so, the already weakened Japanese support of the U.S. policy could erode further and help undermine the American security obligation. The prospect of Taiwan coming under Peking's control would then increase, to the detriment of Japan's security and economic interests. But at present only a minority in Japan is concerned about a mainland takeover.[46] Those analysts worried about this prospect fear regional instability, a shift toward Peking in the regional balance of power, harmful effects on the overseas Chinese, and a stronger PRC naval position athwart Japan's sea lanes.[47]

Another difficulty in any deteriorating situation would be a decision by Taipei to invite the Soviet Union in to shore up Taiwain's position. Though now farfetched, this step was considered plausible by some Japanese scholars in the event that Taipei decided that U.S. and Japanese support was rapidly fading—and, of course, if Moscow were interested.

Worst of all are the possible recriminations that could follow between the United States and Japan should the island fall to Peking.[48] For example, the United States could claim that it did its utmost, only to be undermined by Tokyo's increasingly weak stand; and that, finding itself diplomatically isolated, it was forced to yield when Peking intensified the pressure.

45. The tenuous nature of this favorable scenario is reflected in the tension generated between Taiwan and Japan over the air accord reached by Peking and Tokyo and the position taken by Foreign Minister Ohira that Japan did "not consider the flag marks of the aircraft belonging to Taiwan as something which represented a so-called national flag": *New York Times,* April 25, 1974. Taiwan responded by terminating flights by Japan Air Lines into Taiwan and by China Air Lines into Japan. On the internal political reverberations in Japan, see *New York Times,* April 21, 1974.

46. In February 1970, only 8 percent favored giving arms aid (compared to the question of sending the SDF to Korea) to Taiwan if Communist China attacked the island; 53 percent said no; and 39 percent did not know: Mendel, "Japan's Defense," p. 1056.

47. For a study of Japanese naval defense considerations, see Hideo Sekino, "Japan and Her Maritime Defense," *U.S. Naval Institute Proceedings,* vol. 97 (May 1971), pp. 98–121.

48. Donald C. Hellmann noted the strong economic, historic, and ideological ties between Japan and Taiwan but observed that the Nixon doctrine raised doubts about ultimate U.S. commitments to the region. This in turn, he argued, made it unwise for Japan to abandon its 1969 security obligation to Taiwan and seek some adjustment with Peking. "The Confrontation with *Realpolitik,*" in James W. Morley (ed.), *Forecast for Japan: Security in the 1970's* (Princeton University Press, 1972), pp. 151–60.

U.S. Bases and Facilities in Japan

Even more consistently than the Far East clause, the issue of U.S. bases and other facilities used by U.S. forces has over the years created serious problems in U.S.-Japanese security relations. Bases have proved a continuing source of friction because of inconveniences caused to the Japanese, their link to Vietnam and other external security activities, and their evocation of past defeat and occupation. They have been a ready-made target for all opposition groups anxious to challenge the basis of Japan's foreign policy. With the rekindling of nationalist sentiment in Japan in recent years, the presence of armed foreigners on Japanese soil has become even less tolerable.[49] The fact that the base system represents the repayment for the American security guarantee adds to the strain on the entire relation. With the removal of the issue of Okinawa and with the MST no longer immediately vulnerable as a dangerous entanglement,[50] the opposition has resumed its campaign against the bases.

Scope of the American Establishment

Americans point to the vast reduction in the base system in the home islands since the occupation ended in 1952, from 3,800 installations at that time to 125 in 1970.[51] But to many Japanese, including some analysts committed to the current security policy, the arrangement continues to reflect the structure of the U.S. occupation and requires a thorough overhaul and consolidation.

HOME ISLANDS. Important facilities on the home islands are few in number. For the Army, these are a headquarters complex in Zama and a supply and repair depot in Sagami. The Navy has important bases in Yokosuka and Sasebo and the use of an air facility in Atsugi. The Ma-

---

49. For a description of the leftist opposition campaign against the bases in the late 1960s, see Frank Langdon, "Strains in Current Japanese-American Defense Cooperation," *Asian Survey*, vol. 9 (September 1969), pp. 706–12.

50. For a description of how the government effectively snuffed out the opposition effort to mount a popular mass effort against the MST on the tenth anniversary of the treaty, see Shigeo Ōmori, "June 1970," *Japan Quartely*, vol. 17 (October–December 1970), pp. 383–92.

51. Hearings, p. 1415. For somewhat different figures—2,824 facilities in 1957 and 124 in 1970—see Japan Institute of International Affairs (hereafter JIIA), *White Papers of Japan*, p. 47.

rines use an air facility in Iwakuni, near Sasebo. The Air Force has a major installation in Yokota and in Misawa in the north. (Another northern facility, Chitose, has reverted to Japan.) All except the Iwakuni-Sasebo and Misawa installations are in the Tokyo area. Because Japan is initially responsible for its own defense, twenty-six radar sites are now under Japanese control, though used by the United States. In all, 70 percent of the base area and 77 percent of the U.S. personnel on the four home islands operated within sixty miles of Tokyo in 1972.[52] Under a Kantō Plain consolidation plan, however, many lesser facilities and installations (such as air support and headquarters locations at Fuchū and Tachikawa, the north Fuji firing range, and recreation and housing facilities) reverted to Japan during 1973.[53] In all, eight major installations, five of which are in the Tokyo area, still remain under U.S. control or are available for shared use with the Self-Defense Force.

The naval bases in Yokosuka and Sasebo, along with the Atsugi and Iwakuni air facilities for training, are of significance because they service the Seventh Fleet. Yokosuka is the finest U.S. installation beyond Pearl Harbor and can be considered superior to that base because of the major service facilities supporting it. With several drydocks, one able to accommodate the largest type of aircraft carrier, about 2,000 skilled workers in U.S. employ, and a large depot, it is far superior to Subic Bay in the Philippines, which can handle nothing larger than a 16,000-ton cruiser, or Guam, which lacks large depot facilities.

Sasebo on the western shore also has a large drydock that the Japanese use and that is made available to the United States on seven days' notice.[54] But unlike Yokosuka, no construction takes place there, and the work force is on contract. After deciding to drop Sasebo, the United States reversed its decision in 1969 because of protests from the U.S. Joint Chiefs of Staff. Its strategic location near the Tsushima Strait, the Sea of Japan, and the Yellow Sea, its value during the Korean war, and the absence of an adequate alternate storage facility for petroleum and ammunition were factors affecting the decision to retain the facility.[55]

Apart from Okinawa, on which Marine units are located, the United States does not station ground combat forces in Japan. But the bases

52. Hearings, pp. 1227–30. See also the maps depicting the base system, pp. 1232a–d.
53. *New York Times,* January 24, 1973.
54. Testimony of Rear Admiral Daniel F. Smith, Jr., Hearings, pp. 1235–37.
55. Ibid., pp. 1279–80.

and facilities play an important role in providing area logistical depots, communication sites, naval facilities, air fields for U.S. naval and air force units, and hospitals.

OKINAWA. The bases on Okinawa are of greater magnitude in proportion to the island's size. As of 1970, the United States had invested $750 million in them and controlled 75,000 acres, two-thirds of which was leased annually for a rent of $124 million.[56] Strategically located less than 1,000 miles from Taiwan, Korea, the Philippines, and parts of mainland China, Okinawa provides an excellent close-in staging area and operational base, as well as the best location for stationing a force for quick reaction in the western Pacific. The first combat troops to Vietnam were deployed from the island, and B-52 bombers were refueled in the air over its major air base at Kadena. Air units can move quickly to Korea from Okinawa, which also contains part of the early-warning radar chain that extends from Japan to the Philippines and is the hub of an extensive communication and air-sea transportation net. The capital, Naha, has been used by U.S. air components, and its excellent port facilities underline the island's overall value as a logistical base that can support a deployed force of 500,000 in the Far East. Thus, Okinawa is both a prime target for a considerable consolidation of the U.S. base presence and a major center in the U.S. Asian base system.[57]

Sources of Japanese Opposition

The United States generally has received excellent cooperation in the operation, maintenance, and support of these facilities.[58] Events of recent years, however, add urgency to the question of how rapidly and extensively the United States should proceed with plans for consolidation.[59] Also uncertain is how long—in the face of rising public antagonism and

56. For a discussion of the opposition to, and agitation against, the bases in Okinawa when the reversion issue entered its final diplomatic phases, see Langdon, "Strains," pp. 712–21. At the time of reversion, the United States decided to keep fifty-four bases and turn thirty-four over to the Japanese: Lieutenant Colonel William B. Webb, "Japan's Defense Policy, 1972–1977 and U.S. Military Strategy in East Asia," *National War College Forum* (Summer 1973), p. 62.

57. Testimony of Lieutenant General James B. Lampert, Hearings, pp. 1291–92.

58. Under Secretary of State U. Alexis Johnson, ibid., p. 1152.

59. For example, the Study Committee on National Security Problems called for a realignment and reduction of the bases as part of the process by which the alliance could be placed on a "more equal and more stable basis": "Outlook," p. 4.

increasingly effective exploitation of the base issue by the opposition—effective cooperation can be sustained and at what political price for the Liberal Democratic party.

U.S. VERSUS JAPANESE INTEREST. An important source of tension is the public belief that the bases serve only U.S. interest and represent either a favor bestowed by Japan or a price paid for a security guarantee. This is reinforced by American emphasis on the importance of the bases for U.S. security commitments elsewhere in the Pacific and by the public's attitude that such commitments are extraneous to Japan's needs.[60] The United States has contributed to this problem by stressing—even exaggerating—the non-Japanese orientation of the facilities. A classic case was the testimony before Congress of Under Secretary of State U. Alexis Johnson in January 1970; it made a vivid impression on Japanese experts, who cited his position almost three years later. He noted the importance of the bases to maintain U.S. commitments to Seoul and Taipei and to support U.S. forces in Southeast Asia.[61] Although he did acknowledge the importance of the U.S. naval presence for the security of Japan's sea lanes, the general value of American air strength in the area, and the higher credibility of the U.S. nuclear umbrella given a base presence,[62] he stated that these Japanese installations "are not so much related directly to the defense of Japan and Okinawa as they are to our ability to support our commitments elsewhere."[63]

Johnson, of course, was trying to demonstrate to Congress the increased capacity of a wealthy Japan to bear its own burden of conventional defense. To bow in the direction of Japan's emphasis on autonomous defense also made good political sense. Finally, the main thrust of the testimony centered on the contention that the reversion of Okinawa would not diminish the U.S. capacity to carry out its commitments and that Japan explicitly supported this contention.[64] Nonetheless, for

60. Under Secretary Johnson stated that the Japanese "have tended to think in very self-centered terms of just Japan and only Japan": Hearings, p. 1234.

When asked if American bases were good or bad for Japan, only 14 to 17 percent of Japanese respondents replied affirmatively in polls taken during 1966–70, as against 45 to 61 percent negative answers, and 25 to 37 percent do not know: Mendel, "Japan's Defense," p. 1062.

61. Hearings, p. 1152. Reactions to Johnson's testimony were noted during interviews in August and September 1972.

62. Ibid., pp. 1262 and 1278.

63. Ibid., p. 1166.

64. Ibid., pp. 1166–67.

such an explicitly non-Japanese orientation to be called the primary function of the U.S. facilities was a sting to the Japanese. In fact, until 1969 the Japanese government had followed the opposite tactic, that of justifying the bases publicly on the ground that they were solely for the defense of Japan and avowing that it would not agree to their use for anything else.[65] The impact of this new emphasis, following Satō's conciliatory position on Korea and Taiwan in 1969, led some Japanese scholars and writers to the other extreme, to overlook the many security services the bases continued to perform for Japan.

Many Japanese recognize these security values, but the majority steadfastly believe that the bases are troublesome and unnecessary for Japan.[66] The opposition hammers away at this point and criticizes the wide-ranging American naval operations based on Yokosuka. Erratic U.S. shifts of position on the naval bases have added fuel to the fire. Most unsettling was the navy's indication in 1970 that, under pressure of anticipated budget cuts, it would withdraw from the base at Yokosuka and concentrate at Sasebo.[67] It then reversed its position six months later and made the decision—later also reversed—to leave Sasebo instead. This seemingly cavalier attitude toward important installations, in addition to American determination of major policy decisions on the basis of budget cuts and the lack of any unified base concept, compounded the difficulties, especially because the Japanese placed the highest value on the naval bases. The Satō government naturally continued to avoid public defense of the bases. Coming on the heels of the Nixon doctrine, such behavior led Japanese officials to expect a complete U.S. pullout, and for a while they drafted contingency programs accordingly.[68]

INCONSISTENCY WITH DÉTENTE. The original argument against the bases had held that they were provocative and gave an aggressor a ready excuse to attack Japan.[69] With the emergence of détente, this contention has been supplanted—but not dropped, because it still carries a residual impact—by the argument that the bases, like the MST itself,

---

65. Ibid., p. 1186.
66. See the discussion in Emmerson, *Arms,* p. 95.
67. Shinohara, "National Defense," p. 160.
68. This line of thought lay behind the base evacuation proposals that were developed in 1970 by the Study Committee on National Security Problems.
69. See, for example, the discussion in Shinkichi Etō, "Increasing Japan's Security Capabilities," *Journal of Social and Political Ideas of Japan,* vol. 4 (August 1966).

have become unnecessary.[70] Another potent thesis holds that they affront Japanese nationalism and prevent the country from acting as an independent power.[71] Although this allegation can be challenged by reference not only to the experience of European allies but also to recent Japanese initiatives toward Peking and Moscow, the argument persists that the bases do generate constraints, that Japan cannot operate with the freedom enjoyed by West Germany and other European nations that host American bases.

The bases are criticized also for weakening the durability of the MST. Because the facilities provide the primary motivation for anti-American feelings, it is argued, their elimination would put the MST on a sounder political footing and convert the alliance essentially into a nuclear guarantee, with important psychological benefit to Japan in negotiations with the communist powers. A related view holds that the popular feeling against the bases will continue to grow and thus lead to an ever widening gap between the government and the people. The best solution, therefore, would be to decrease the military character of the MST by diminishing the bases.[72] This view recognizes that Japan and China may be on a course of competition or even confrontation in Asia, but it holds nonetheless that a policy of relying on U.S. bases to protect Japan's interests cannot endure.

Contributing to arguments against continuation of the bases is the belief that the bases no longer are crucial to maintain the credibility of the nuclear umbrella, especially in a period of détente.[73] A related complaint is that by demanding so elaborate a base structure, the United States requires of Japan too great a return for this nuclear guarantee.

70. The *Yomiuri* poll of June 1969 found that of the 50 percent who did not think that Japan needed U.S. military bases, about one-third gave as their reason that the bases would cause Japan's involvement in war. In 1970 a similar percentage of the opponents of the bases also gave as their reason fear of involvement in war: Mendel, "Japan's Defense," p. 1063.

71. Study Committee on National Security Problems, "Outlook," p. 17.

72. See, for example, Etō, "Increasing Japan's Security Capabilities," and Yōnosuke Nagai, "Japan's Foreign Policy Objective in a Nuclear Milieu," *JSPIJ*, vol. 5 (April 1967), pp. 27–43. Although he rejected the argument that the U.S. tie made Japan a target, Nagai argued for a more limited MST that would allow Japan to be quasi-neutral and to follow an independent course. The idea of diminishing the military-base character of the MST arrangement permeates the work of the Study Committee on National Security Problems.

73. The Study Committee on National Security Problems summarizes arguments against the bases: "Outlook," p. 17. It also points out the extent to which technological developments reduced the value and need for the bases: ibid., p. 14.

Such U.S. insistence, some defense experts argue, could precipitate a dramatic Japanese public reaction.

INTERNAL SOCIAL AND POLITICAL AGGRAVATION. Compounding these general political difficulties have been specific physical inconveniences and disturbances to Japanese life, already suffering under conditions of overcrowding and rapid urbanization and industrialization. The encroachment of cities on what were once outlying areas raises assorted problems of safety, lack of space, noise, pollution, unavailability of land to powerful real estate interests, and the crowding of Japan's air and maritime transport facilities.[74] Cases in point include the overcrowding of Naha air field, the spread of Tokyo toward Yokota, and the desire of Japan to use land and water facilities in the Yokosuka area and of the Japanese people to use dwellings occupied by U.S. personnel. A variety of incidents, accidental or deliberately precipitated, have plagued U.S.-Japanese relations in recent years. Even those Japanese who are anxious to maintain the base system call for a greater sensitivity to Japanese needs.

The election of socialist mayors and prefectural governors has added legitimate local support to the opponents' position.[75] These officials have sought legal means to harass or close the bases. The invoking of local transport laws in mid-1972 to block the transport of tanks from Sagami to the port of Yokohama for shipment to Vietnam reflected this trend. Under the Status of Forces Agreement (SOFA) of 1960, the United States is obliged to obey regulations; but Japan also is required to facilitate the operation of the bases.[76] The government moved cautiously over a period of weeks; finally it waived technical rules and allowed the tanks to be moved, although it expressed the hope that the Sagami facility would not be used for such purposes in the future and that eventually it would revert to Japan.

74. In the *Yomiuri* poll of June 1969, 20 percent of those opposed to bases cited pollution and the numerous disputes caused by the existence of the bases; the NHK (Japanese Broadcasting Corporation) poll of September 1969 found 33 percent of those opposed were troubled by the public hazard the bases posed; in 1970, Mendel noted that 30 percent mentioned nuisances caused by bases: "Japan's Defense," p. 1064.

75. For two studies in the 1960s on the evolution of local politics and especially the governorship of prefectures, see Bradley M. Richardson, "Japanese Local Politics: Support Mobilization and Leadership Styles," *Asian Survey*, vol. 7 (December 1967), pp. 860–75; and Young C. Kim, "Gubernatorial Elections in Japan," *Asian Survey*, vol. 8 (August 1968), pp. 646–65.

76. The SOFA went into effect on January 14, 1960, the same year that the MST went into effect. SOFA operations are reviewed annually by Congress and appear as reports of the Senate Committee on Armed Services.

Problems of this type stem, to some extent, from a limited American grasp of detailed local regulations, but essentially they reflect an intent to harass. Such matters the United States regards as internal Japanese issues, but Tokyo does not want to expend any large amount of political capital in protecting American base interests. On the other hand, the Japanese government realizes that the United States now opposes a revised MST that would remove Japan's obligation to provide facilities.

Potential Methods of Consolidation

Both governments therefore favor consolidating and reducing bases to meet Japan's political needs and U.S. operational requirements. The most extreme solution would be a complete evacuation of all facilities, modified by arrangements to have U.S. forces return in an emergency. But many officials and scholars argue that Japan cannot renege on its only obligation under the treaty. In their view, even if bases were made available for American use in an emergency, the United States still would view the suggestion of such an arrangement by the Japanese as trying to get something for nothing.

RESTRUCTURED BASE SYSTEMS. A minimal base system would provide for one naval base, Yokosuka, and one air base, Yokota, for example, or shared use of Atsugi. Arrangements also could be made for joint use of other facilities that would be turned over to the SDF, though satisfactory joint operations admittedly are difficult to sustain. One politically attractive proposal that would not negate American capabilities calls for fewer air bases and for locating them in sparsely populated areas. It calls also for retention of the Sasebo and Yokosuka naval bases but for the removal to the north of all air facilities. This would mean evacuation from the Tokyo area (Atsugi and Yokota) and from Iwakuni, near a projected express rail line.[77] There is still no great public pressure for such wholesale removal from the vicinity of Tokyo, although the United States acknowledges that Yokota presents a noise and hazard problem.[78]

The American position generally has been to agree to a reduction and consolidation of the base system but not to yield important facilities in the Kantō Plain in the vicinity of Tokyo. The United States has held that continued gradual progress, as in the 1969–70, 1972–73, and 1974

77. Hearings, p. 1264.
78. See, for example, the testimony of Scott George, ibid., p. 1251.

arrangements regarding the Kantō area and Okinawa, provides sufficient response to the desires of the Japanese public.[79] Many Japanese believe that, with the Vietnam war over, the issue will recede, especially if the general level of tension in the Far East continues to decline. Furthermore, a streamlined base system that can be depicted as a crucial factor in stability and détente in East Asia might gain greater public acceptance. Because the base system assures continuous American military cooperation and counteracts American domestic pressures toward isolationism, the Japanese government itself does not want it dismantled.[80] Some defense officials would favor having Japan pay offsetting costs to keep the bases, but they recognize that such an action is politically impossible.

Thus, the issues boil down to what type of consolidation, how to effect it, and with what rationalized concept to present it to the Japanese public. The major problem with placing air bases away from settled areas is the need to pair air and naval installations for maximum value to the carrier forces. In this sense, Atsugi-Yokosuka and Iwakuni-Sasebo each constitutes a packet that is difficult to fragment. It has been observed that the citizens around Atsugi preferred it to remain as an SDF base with American usage rather than to become a civilian facility whose commercial jet traffic would be heavier and noisier. Of the four bases, Iwakuni presents the greatest problem because its value relative to Korea and Southeast Asia is offset by the difficulty of planning rail movement. One solution would be for the United States to give way on Sasebo and Iwakuni, thus reducing pressure against other bases, especially the continued use of Yokota and the shared use of Atsugi along with Yokosuka. Necessary changes on Okinawa, especially the overcrowded Naha region, were begun during the consolidation of 1973, but they still have a way to go.[81]

79. Note particularly the consolidation plan announced early in 1973 (*New York Times,* January 24, 1973) and the consolidation plan for Okinawa agreed on in January 1974 (*Asahi,* January 30 and February 2, 1974).

80. Kohtani, "Prospects," p. 10. On the other hand, the Study Committee on National Security Problems felt that the best way to meet a resurgence of U.S. neo-isolationism was to progress further on the withdrawal from the bases: "Outlook," pp. 5, 10–11.

81. Because of the emotional aspects of reversion and because of the extensive U.S. facilities in Okinawa, Japanese public opinion was even more hostile to a post-reversion continuation of bases there than in the home islands, according to polls taken before the completion of reversion in 1972. In 1970, only 20 percent

In addition to particular problems such as location in populated areas (for example, Yokota), overcrowding (Naha), specific functions (Sagami), conflicting needs (Iwakuni), and base combinations (Yokosuka-Atsugi and Sasebo-Iwakuni), the two sides may differ over general base patterns. The Japanese prefer the fewest number, preferably one or two for each critical military function, consolidated into extensive installations. To take a hypothetical example, these could include Kaneda and Misawa as air bases and Yokosuka as a naval installation. But what the Japanese would consider unnecessary duplication would appear to the United States as providing essential flexibility; and the U.S. forces, with their complex and numerous missions, may judge that a larger number of smaller installations creates a more dependable system.

MUTUAL ACCEPTANCE OF CONSOLIDATION. Questions of the pace of consolidation are equally important. In having failed to rationalize its holdings long ago, the United States can be accused of dilatory responses to evident Japanese needs. But action under compulsion, in response to Japanese pressures, would neither improve relations nor bode well for the future stability of the base system. A willingness to act without duress and according to a mutually acceptable overall plan could ameliorate matters considerably. But given the Japanese urge to reduce the U.S. base presence, any concessions might lead inexorably to a new series of targets. From this perspective, the United States should give ground only grudgingly, since easy conciliation would only intensify the pressure.

This leads to the question of whether Washington and Tokyo should agree on a unified concept that each could defend in public or continue to allow the political marketplace to regulate change. A revised joint approach, one that justifies the system under new international conditions, appears attractive. This would make the Japanese government an open advocate and defender of the revised system. On the other hand, given their divergent political needs and military perspectives, the two sides might be unable to reach any comprehensive arrangement. Even

favored continuing the bases, 59 percent opposed, and 21 percent did not know: Mendel, "Japan's Defense," p. 1063.

For a general review of the diplomatic and local issues involved in the reversion, see Makoto Takizawa, "Okinawa: Reversion to Japan and Future Prospects," *Asian Survey*, vol. 11 (May 1971), pp. 496–505. The Study Committee on National Security Problems gave urgent priority to the reduction of the U.S. force and base presence on Okinawa: "Outlook," pp. 20–22. A further modest reduction of the U.S. system on Okinawa—seven small facilities and portions of sixteen others —was reported in the *New York Times,* January 31, 1974.

should they succeed, a public presentation would become an immediate target for further modifications; and any confidential arrangement would stand a good chance of being leaked in Tokyo. Nevertheless, a unified, agreed-upon concept, coupled with a firm joint position on consolidation, may be preferable to the intermittent pressures for change that characterize affairs at present.

An ancillary question is whether to announce agreed-upon changes gradually or a drastic reduction all at once. The first approach appeases the populace, demonstrates continued progress, preserves the core of the system, and gains time. Its defect lies in not coming to grips with the need to gain widespread and immediate public approval, which a dramatic adjustment might do. Such a move could provide great concessions yet serve as a warning to the Japanese public that further opposition could jeopardize the entire defense relation. On the other hand, a dramatic elimination of as many bases as feasible could have the negative effect of bringing the remaining, vital bases into the foreground as potential new targets of the opposition. Such a step also might bring the MST itself into question and intensify concern about the durability of the U.S. commitment.[82]

Bureaucratic problems also complicate the transfer of bases. For example, the U.S. Department of Defense has displayed considerable rigidity in trying to adhere to the terms of the agreement far beyond the political point of no return. Another derives from the stipulation in the U.S.-Japanese agreement that Japan supply the United States with equivalent facilities and finance relocation should the United States declare such a need to exist. Base reductions or reversions thus can be delayed or checked by lack of equivalent substitutes, the cost of relocation, or sometimes the requirement that the SDF assume tasks previously American held.[83] Even when recovered base land is so valuable that Tokyo realizes a net gain despite relocation costs, it is often difficult to translate this into budgetary terms so as to balance appropriations itemized for relocation expenses.[84] This relates in part to Japan's ponderously

---

82. A somewhat different argument appears in the recent writings of Junnosuke Kishida, who holds that the credibility of the "worldwide nuclear umbrella" erected by the two superpowers is high and stable, but that it is done voluntarily on their part and neither relies on any particular security arrangement nor requires any price from the allies: "Japan's Non-Nuclear Policy," *Survival*, vol. 15 (January–February 1973), pp. 17–18.

83. Hearings, p. 1277.

84. Ibid., p. 1239.

bureaucratic budgetary process, which requires that U.S. relocation requests be put forward only at the proper time in the budgetary cycle.

The U.S. Force Presence

The question of whether U.S. forces should be stationed in Japan logically would seem to be a function of the base issue. The Japanese, however, respond less negatively to this issue than to that of the facilities. They perceive the U.S. force as playing a more direct role in their security—adding to the credibility of deterrence and defending Japan in certain contingencies—than do the installations. And the bases and forces of the Seventh Fleet are far more acceptable than air and army units and bases.

The Japanese Capability

Japanese defense planners foresee a combat role, under certain contingencies, for U.S. air and naval forces stationed in Japan despite the U.S. position that American forces "are not primarily there for direct defense of Japan's home islands themselves but to carry out other treaty commitments in the area which also involve Japanese security."[85] Thus, in 1966 a National Defense Council staff paper foresaw that Japan would provide for its own security against large-scale disorders, a war of national liberation, and even low-level assaults such as guerrilla infiltrations or probing attacks. It recognized, however, that substantial air attacks and interdiction of Japanese shipping, to say nothing of a full-scale conventional assault, could be met effectively only with American help.[86] Japan has a significant air defense establishment but only a modest supply of ammunition. Because the Maritime Self-Defense Force (MSDF) is effective only in coastal and nearby waters, Japan can cope with attacks on shipping only in these regions and depends on the U.S. Navy to keep the sea lanes open. With less than a one-month supply of material to deal with a large-scale attack, Japan would need immediate U.S. help to contain such a threat and a fairly rapid and large-scale U.S. intervention to repel it.[87]

85. Ibid., p. 1214.
86. Weinstein, "Defense Policy," p. 170.
87. Shinohara notes that the departure of U.S. forces would leave Japan in a

A dispute apparently exists in Japanese defense circles as to whether the United States will be willing to fight a conventional war in the future to defend even so important an ally as Japan.[88] But above the level of a small-scale attack, Japan clearly cannot assume primary responsibility for its external defense with its present force, despite its formal agreement to do so. Current SDF strength compels a would-be attacker only to act on a scale large enough to invoke the MST and, presumably, an American response. The American element in this conventional combat scenario thus represents a deterrent whose credibility would be reinforced by a continued U.S. air and naval presence in Japan. Such forces become more important as a general force reduction in Asia creates doubt about the U.S. commitment.[89] Adding to the uncertainty, the Nixon doctrine has been misinterpreted as suggesting that the United States would act only against a nuclear threat and not against a conventional threat by a nuclear power above a level that the SDF could handle. But the Nixon statement explicitly committed the United States to meet just such conventional attacks by nuclear powers. With U.S. forces gone, the Japanese might well conclude, despite such American statements to the contrary, that the United States expected its allies to cope with all nonnuclear threats presented by a nuclear power without substantial U.S. help.[90] Despite considerable talk of autonomous defense, the Japanese, even if they upgrade their defense effort considerably, will not attain that capability during the next decade.

The Concept of Emergency Stationing

But the desire to end the U.S. force presence continues to be strengthened by the drawdown of U.S. forces in Japan and by authoritative American statements earmarking these units for security requirements elsewhere in Asia.[91] The concept of a troop withdrawal but return in an

---

position in which it would be hard pressed to defend itself: "National Defense," p. 160. See also Momoi, "Japan's Defense Policies," pp. 105–06.

88. Such doubts are implicit in the discussion of the new strategic plan, *New York Times*, March 4, 1973. See also editorial note in *Survival*, vol. 15 (July–August 1973), p. 184.

89. Shinohara, "National Defense," p. 160.

90. Emmerson, *Arms*, pp. 392–93; and Junnosuke Kishida, "Non-Nuclear Japan: Her National Security and Role for Peace in Asia" (paper prepared for Peace in Asia conference, Kyoto, Japan, June 1972; processed), p. 2.

91. As of the early 1970s, U.S. forces in Japan proper totaled 25,000 in contrast to the 200,000 at the end of the Korean war and 70,000 in 1956: Webb,

emergency and at Japan's request (if for no other reason than to prevent a massive buildup of the SDF once the Americans left), combined with proposals for treaty revisions providing for Japan's autonomous defense, was reiterated during the 1960s.[92] These ideas have attracted more widespread attention in recent years, as the United States seemed to be turning inward and as the Japanese themselves displayed less tolerance of alien military forces.[93]

If Japan now fosters the notion of emergency stationing only and claims, unrealistically, that projected improvements in the Self-Defense Forces will enable it to provide for its own conventional defense, some major problems may emerge. Based on projections of the fourth defense plan, the SDF clearly remains unable to cope with conventional defense needs.[94] Therefore, those who oppose extensive rearmament for Japan hold that an American evacuation will bring on irresistible internal pressures for major augmentation of the Japanese defense capability.[95] They foresee difficulty with a powerful Soviet Union, the rapid modernization of Peking's forces, and growing uncertainty about the American commitment all driving Japan inexorably toward major rearmament, even in a period of détente.[96]

Other issues concern the availability of the bases and the feasibility of U.S. reentry in time of crisis. Some defense experts argue that unless the

---

"Japan's Defense Policy," p. 49. A drop during 1973 from 64,000 to 56,000 on Okinawa was reported in the *New York Times,* January 31, 1974.

92. The concept of emergency stationing was first proposed, by the Democratic Socialist party, during Diet debates in 1959–60 over revision of the 1952 treaty. The party's plank in 1965 called for "a security treaty without the stationing of troops in peacetime." See Nagai, "Japan's Foreign Policy," pp. 36–37 and 41.

93. The Study Committee on National Security Problems held that the removal of an American force presence would improve the image of the security tie with the Japanese public: "Outlook," p. 16. As recently as 1973, the argument in favor of emergency stationing was strongly advocated by Muraoka, "Japanese Security," pp. 10 and 22.

94. Momoi even notes the difficulties Japan would have in the 1970s in coping with insurgency especially if augmented by sea-borne support activities: "Japan's Defense Policies," p. 112.

95. In a speech, Secretary of State William Rogers reassured the Japanese of the validity of the U.S. security tie and noted that a U.S. military withdrawal would lead Japan to rearm. *New York Times,* April 24, 1973.

96. Of course, many persons who are fundamentally opposed to the present course of Japan's foreign policy argue even more forcefully that U.S. credibility is disappearing, but then go on to advocate a near pacifist foreign policy of curtailed rearmament and nonaggression treaties with Moscow and Peking. See, for example, Yoshikazu Sakamoto, "A New Foreign Policy," *Japan Quarterly,* vol. 19 (July–September 1972), pp. 272 and 276.

United States leaves supporting forces at the bases, an effective return in time of emergency would be impossible. The need for adequate planning, coordination, and adjustment to new technology and to new contingencies also weigh against a complete evacuation. And given the pressure for civilian control and use of bases, many facilities may be lost to the SDF.[97] The balance of forces in Japanese politics and fear of militarism lurking behind a large base complex make this arrangement even more problematic.

Finally, the emergency stationing proposal is essentially unequal. The United States would lose use of the bases while remaining obliged to protect Japan; and the Tokyo government would determine when and whether to ask for the reentry of U.S. forces, which then must respond.[98] Such a request obviously would come only during a deep crisis and would be certain to heighten tension and reduce the likelihood that either party would act constructively. The proposal rests on the shaky premise that an alliance can be diluted radically in normal times and yet engender effective cooperation in an emergency.

Areas of Potential Compromise

If a U.S. force is to remain in Japan, how can this be made mutually acceptable without a debilitating effect on the entire alliance? The psychological objective, essentially a task for the Tokyo government, is to heighten the perception on the part of the Japanese public that these units serve Japan's security interests. Any deployment of forces therefore should represent a response to a Japanese desire rather than an American demand. Withdrawals of U.S. forces in recent years have led to more realistic Japanese consideration of national security needs, and the general reduction of tensions in Asia permits a more judicious appraisal of the matter. Perhaps all the government can do is clarify for its people the extent of Japan's inability to provide for its own defense, explain the direct security contribution of U.S forces, and depict the staggering increase in the SDF that would be required if Japan is actually to provide

97. In fact, the Study Committee on National Security Problems recommended that some bases be turned over to private use: "Outlook," p. 8.

98. By contrast, the Study Committee on National Security Problems argues that emergency stationing would be effective, that standing arrangements could be made to establish in advance a system of prompt aid. It does recognize that considerable joint U.S.-Japanese defense planning is required on the quantitative and qualitative nature of the move, on who would decide that an emergency exists, and on the necessary legislative measures: "Outlook," pp. 17 and 24.

for its own conventional defense.[99] The atmosphere of détente, the rise of nationalist sentiment, and the political value of the stress on Japan's self-reliance make this approach difficult even for a determined and persistent government.

On the whole, a sizable cutback in American forces, but one measurably short of complete evacuation, may offer the best solution. A smaller, elite force of naval, air, and support-element specialists would be better behaved, thereby reducing irritants even further. The Japanese actually have treated the United States very favorably thus far in implementing the SOFA of 1960. They have been lenient in prosecution of arrested Americans[100] and have not raised technical obstacles or difficulties on a wide variety of issues, ranging from post exchange privileges for retired military personnel to sovereign command of air fields.

Some American concessions to national sensitivities that would place Tokyo on a par with Bonn—but without requiring a comparable agreement on purchases of U.S. military equipment to offset costs to the United States of keeping forces abroad—could further improve the public's attitude toward American forces in Japan. From one perspective, the continued American force and base presence over so long a period of time is a remarkable achievement, considering that the foreign protectors on its soil were originally occupiers. More judicious arrangements will be required to sustain the relation.

Crucial to a continued U.S. naval presence is the broad acceptance, among defense experts and the informed public, of the importance of the Seventh Fleet to Japan's security. Even some political analysts strongly opposed to a continued force and base presence acknowledge that a U.S. naval evacuation would harm Japan's vital interests.[101] To most defense analysts, the Seventh Fleet is a keystone of peace and security in the Far East. Given the continuing growth of Soviet naval power and the antici-

99. For example, the 1970–71 abstract of the 1970 Japan Defense Agency defense plan briefly and clearly depicts, with map and figures, the extent to which unidentified air and naval ships have been active in the seas and skies around Japan: JIIA, *White Papers of Japan*, pp. 46–47.

100. In 1969–70, for example, 3,305 cases were waived, released, or dropped; there were 445 convictions, with confinement in only 20 cases. *Operation of Article VII, NATO Status of Forces Treaty*, Report of the Committee on Armed Services, U.S. Senate, 92 Cong. 2 sess. (March 17, 1972), p. 7.

101. See, for example, Kishida, "Non-Nuclear Japan," p. 2. This appraisal of the acceptability of the Seventh Fleet was a consistent theme through almost all of the interviews conducted by the author during July and September 1972.

pated development of a nuclear-powered navy by Peking, these analysts feel that the Seventh Fleet is essential to their security even if the Sino-Soviet split persists.[102] Without it, they argue, Japan would have to build its own deepwater navy. Even many opponents of the base system and of the military aspects of the MST expect naval bases to remain. They limit their demands to reductions in American use of the facilities, number of ships, and frequency of visits. Certain journalists and academic critics argue that Japan could live with communist-dominated sea lanes or that the Seventh Fleet is of ambiguous value, since much depends on the still unclear intention behind the Soviet naval buildup. Most, however, accept its value and see it as underscoring U.S. credibility, protecting vital sea lanes, increasing the security of Korea and other Asian states, and generating far fewer base problems than the other branches of the armed forces.

This judgment is reinforced by the generally favorable response in the Japanese press in the fall of 1972 to the U.S.-Japanese decision to make Yokosuka a home port for U.S. carriers.[103] Of major importance was the international context, especially the winding down of the war in Vietnam, which led the Japanese press to conclude that the U.S. base structure in Japan no longer would serve as a rear support for that war. Rather, they now saw it as an underpinning for the strategic deterrent force and as part of a complex of Pacific bases to protect Northeast Asia. The press also noted that Japan's contingency plans, which need the U.S. carriers to counter any major attack from the north, now enjoyed greater credibility. Finally, indicating that the idea of U.S. forces as valuable hostages had not died but probably had lost its value because of troop withdrawals, the newspapers noted that the presence in Yokosuka of the American families of carrier crews would ensure a U.S. military response to an attack on Japan.

102. See, for example, Kohtani, "Prospects," pp. 11–12; and Osamu Kaihara, "Real Character of the U.S.-Japan Security Treaty as Is Seen in the Fourth Defense Power Consolidation Plan," *Asia* (May 1972). Webb, in "Japan's Defense Policy," pp. 53–54, stresses Japan's maritime vulnerability, noting that eighty ships a day drop anchor at Japanese ports and unload 900,000 tons of supplies daily. The Soviet Far Eastern fleet contains 120 submarines, about half of which are attack boats; 27 others have ballistic missiles and 24 have subsonic cruise missiles.

103. This became a public issue when the government sent a note to the mayor of Yokosuka with regard to the home porting of a carrier on November 16, 1972. The comments of the leading Tokyo newspapers—*Mainichi*, *Yomiuri*, and *Asahi*—of November 17 to 19 indicated a cautious reaction, mild to favorable, and a somewhat cautious acceptance of the home porting concept.

In conclusion, it seems desirable for the United States to reduce its forces and bases to the greatest extent possible, thus preserving valuable foreign exchange, lowering the frequency of disturbing incidents, and reducing social and political problems. By agreeing to keep some U.S. air and naval forces in Japan and by use of the home port arrangement, the United States would retain its deterrent credibility against both conventional and nuclear threats.[104] Japan in turn would still feel that it was reciprocating sufficiently in security matters; in fact, the Japanese look upon the home port agreement as a responsive way of carrying more of the defense burden. By maintaining adequate naval facilities, the United States also would assure other of its allies that the force and base reductions in Japan did not foreshadow U.S. abandonment of them.[105]

Prior Consultation

Although it is tied to the issue of U.S. bases, the issue of prior consultation at first generated little public debate, but it has gained importance in recent years. The Japanese government has now expressed an interest in defining combat operations—which do require consultation—more carefully than in the past; in achieving more general control over Japan-based U.S. operations in the Pacific; and in closer monitoring of routine U.S. activities at the bases themselves. Toward the end of the Satō regime Foreign Minister Fukuda, with these objectives in mind, went on record at the Security Consultation Committee (the senior U.S.-Japanese body for overseeing the security relation) as desiring a review of the manner in which prior consultation has operated. As yet the Japanese have made no specific proposals and probably are still sorting out what they wish to control. In the future, this previously quiescent matter could become a formidable problem in bilateral security relations.

104. The persistence of the credibility problem is evident in the doubts raised on both levels by a professor at the National Defense College, Tokyo: Momoi, "Japan's Defense Policies," p. 113.

105. It might also help to counter the recurrent argument that the United States is more likely to keep forces in Europe while withdrawing from East Asia, and that a decision against a European withdrawal might even force an accelerated withdrawal from Asia. These concerns were expressed by the Study Committee of National Security Problems, "Outlook," pp. 12–13.

Current Bilateral Understanding of "Combat Operations"

The U.S.-Japanese exchange of notes in 1960 committed the United States to consult with Japan before it could make major changes in the deployment of U.S. forces to Japan or in their combat equipment, or before it could use Japanese bases for combat operations undertaken from Japan.[106] Most of the difficulties relate to the latter condition, although the entire subject was handled so loosely that no written understanding exists to define the requirements for prior consultation even in the first category. The Japanese themselves offered details, which the United States then tacitly accepted. In terms of force changes, sizes requiring consultation are one army division, one naval task force, or one air force division of seventy-five fighter-bombers. In equipment, it means nuclear weapons, intermediate and long-range missiles, or the construction of missile sites or launchers.[107]

It has been alleged that, whereas Japan interprets prior consultation as meaning prior Japanese approval, the United States considers it to mean merely informing Japan of actions to be taken in these categories. But the latter is not the case, since authoritative U.S. statements have indicated that the 1960 arrangement gives Japan a veto in these matters.[108] The United States understands prior consultation to mean Japanese agreement before any of the enumerated actions can be undertaken: the communiqué of January 19, 1960, states that "the United States government has no intention of acting in a manner contrary to the wishes of the Japanese government." In a sense, Satō's elaborate 1969 concession in promising favorable consideration to a U.S. request for use of the bases to defend Korea reflects the expectations of both parties that the United States would honor its commitment to secure Japan's consent before using the bases for combat operations outside of Japan.

But despite the far-flung activities of the Seventh Fleet and the use of Japanese facilities for the war in Vietnam, the United States never has sought Japan's agreement to any of its activities—nor has Japan sought to invoke prior consultation in any instance. "There has been no occasion since the Treaty went into effect under which the United States has

106. See the discussion in Emmerson, *Arms,* pp. 80–81.
107. Ibid., pp. 86–87.
108. Statement by Under Secretary of State U. A. Johnson in response to a question posed in his backgrounder of November 21, 1969: Hearings, p. 1442. See also his interchange with Senator Stuart Symington, ibid., p. 1178.

asked for consultations in accordance with this understanding," according to Under Secretary of State U. Alexis Johnson.[109]

The explanation lies in the literal interpretation of the term "combat operations." The Japanese government itself has stressed that it does not mean simply going into a combat area. Rather, combat operations requiring prior consultation means the U.S. use of a Japanese base for launching actual combat actions: for example, an aircraft taking off from a Japanese base to bomb another area or troops embarking from Japan to go directly into combat.[110] Similarly, a plane or ship dispatched on a mission would be involved in combat and so come under the consultation rule, as would any naval vessel or aircraft receiving orders, while in Japan, to engage in combat.[111]

On the other hand, if a ship leaves port and then is ordered into combat, prior consultation is unnecessary. The same applies to forces going to a combat zone but not engaging directly in combat upon arrival, as well as to the supply of food or materials to a combat zone. In fact, all naval vessels, including nuclear-powered ones, are free to come and go.[112] Nor has Japan made an issue of naval vessels calling at U.S. bases in Japan en route to or from a combat zone. Also escaping scrutiny are aircraft in or passing through Japan or being transferred elsewhere in order eventually to engage in combat.[113] Nor are various kinds of limited operations, other than reprisal, subject to scrutiny; these include aircraft dispatched to rescue vessels or other planes on the high seas—for example, cases similar to the North Korean shootdown of an EC-121 aircraft in 1969 and capture of the destroyer *Pueblo* in 1968— or to serve as escorts in such situations.[114] Reconnaissance and armed support of such limited activities also may be undertaken without prior consultation.

In sum, combat operations is "implicitly understood by both governments . . . to mean clearly and specifically an American aircraft taking off from a Japanese base, bombing another area, and coming back to a

109. In the opening statement before the Senate subcommittee, ibid., p. 1416.
110. Emmerson, *Arms,* p. 88; and Hearings, p. 1416.
111. Emmerson, *Arms,* p. 89.
112. Under 1964 and 1967 agreements regarding submarines and surface vessels, respectively, the United States, to alleviate apprehension regarding the safety of these ships, has elected to discuss the entry of nuclear-powered vessels with Japan prior to exercising the right of entry to port: Hearings, p. 1419.
113. Ibid., pp. 1416 and 1155–57.
114. Ibid., p. 1416.

Japanese base. Otherwise, movements of forces, movements of aircraft, movements of ships not involving mounting combat operations directly from Japan are not involved and do not require consultation or agreement by both governments."[115]

Prospects for Greater Japanese Control

This application of the understanding clearly has placed little restriction on the U.S. freedom to operate from Japanese bases. Vessels and planes are free to engage directly in combat operations upon leaving Japan, provided they receive explicit orders only after departure. Deployments to combat zones are permissible as long as combat assignments come after arrival. And many combat-support operations—intelligence, logistical, or escort—do not require clearance. It is little wonder that the Japanese want to explore a more restrictive definition of what is and is not a combat operation. Because this issue relates to U.S. rights under the Far East clause of the MST, any such change in understanding could lead to efforts to restrict the meaning of "peace and security in the Far East" and to redefine the region more narrowly—for example, by excluding Taiwan.

POTENTIAL JAPANESE STRATEGIES. As in many other instances, the Japanese are approaching these broader questions gradually. They seek first to use the right of prior consultation to get more information about, and greater control over, routine American base operations. Then eventually they may move toward regulating use of Japanese bases to support American peacetime activities in the Pacific and toward a wider interpretation of combat operations. Japan also may assert the initiative—heretofore assumed to be an American prerogative, though never exercised—under Article VI to seek prior consultation on the use of bases. In discussing activities at the bases, Japan could take issue with those with which they disagree. In principle, Foreign Minister Fukuda adopted this point, long advocated by the Japanese Socialist party, when he asserted Japan's interest in reviewing the entire consultative process.

By having close and "continuing," as well as "prior," consultation and by taking the lead in raising specific inquiries, the Japanese would seek to become better informed about all activities at the bases. This would require more comprehensive U.S. reports on these activities,

---

115. Under Secretary Johnson in backgrounder, November 21, 1969: ibid., p. 1445.

which the government could then relay to the Diet. As the legislative sessions of 1972 demonstrated, the opposition will concentrate on defense-related issues, especially the base question. The United States must reach agreement within its own ranks on what to report and whether to present as complete a statement as possible. The Japanese interest in thorough coverage of all activities stems from a passion for detailed information and from the opposition belief that the more it learns—and the more negative publicity it can generate—the greater the harm to security ties. The Japanese cabinet, however, may not desire full coverage, thereby escaping the potentially embarrassing consequences of the complete divulgence required of the government. On the U.S. side, the military attitude holds that, for American flexibility and maneuverability, the less reported the better. Thus, what to report and how present complications both in bilateral relations and for each government.

PROBLEMS OF MONITORING U.S. ACTIVITIES. Problems are bound to arise even under the favorable conditions of peace and détente. Home porting a carrier signifies a considerable increase in aircraft training exercises in Japan: it intensifies the issue of noise pollution and increases the need for a naval air station in the crowded Kantō Plain area. In addition, the Seventh Fleet, however highly regarded, could attract intense criticism should any disclosure occur of wide-ranging operations and possible involvement in future crises beyond the scope of Japanese interests. Detailed disclosures in times of stress also can give rise to accusations of American engagement in combat-related activities without prior consultation.

The monitoring of U.S. operations by means of prior and continuing consultation thus could lead to sharp policy differences.[116] Motivated by desires to improve relations with China, to gain some distance from an increasingly less reliable American ally, and to respond to a nationalist sentiment that pervades the bureaucracy as well as the public, Japan may try to curtail American extraterritorial activities. Washington and Tokyo could disagree about what constitutes acceptable activities, with Japan trying to make U.S. behavior conform to its standards. Persistent Japanese efforts could fundamentally change the entire security relation.

116. The Study Committee on National Security Problems wished to add discussions of the modalities for "emergency stationing" to the list of topics requiring prior consultation: "Outlook," p. 24.

But its deep fear of the consequences of Soviet naval dominance of the western Pacific remains a major restraint on Tokyo. Having already experienced an unpleasant false alarm over a U.S. naval cutback in the wake of the Nixon doctrine during 1970, the Japanese government is anxious not to jeopardize the long-term presence of American naval power in its home waters.

ISSUES INVOLVING NUCLEAR WEAPONS. Two questions have arisen concerning the requirement for consultation before the introduction of nuclear weapons into Japan. One involves the leeway for the United States to bring in such weapons under American control in an emergency. During the session of the Diet in 1971 considering the return of Okinawa, Prime Minister Satō espoused as official policy three negative commitments that reflected a long-standing Japanese position regarding nuclear weapons: not to have Japan possess them, not to manufacture them, and not to have them brought in. These commitments represented part of his tactic to gain support of the opposition Komeito and Democratic Socialist party for the Okinawa treaty. Considering the matter in the spring of 1972, LDP security specialists saw no difficulty with the first two commitments, but they questioned whether the third did not seriously weaken the guarantee effects of the U.S. nuclear umbrella.[117] They wanted to keep open the possibility that the United States could bring in such weapons in an emergency, following prior consultation. Although recognizing that the critical weapons of strategic deterrence and guarantee must remain outside Japan, they viewed tactical needs quite differently. Specifically, Soviet military exercises at sea in recent years have stressed landing operations, including the simulated use of nuclear weapons. This could make the role of tactical nuclear weapons for the defense of Japan of critical importance in countermeasures against aircraft as well as warships and seaborne assault vessels.[118] The Soviets are not believed to possess a significant amphibious attack capability at present, but this inadequacy could be overcome after 1975. Doubt therefore exists regarding the wisdom of adopting in advance a mandatory obliga-

117. This point was made by the LDP's Security Problems Research Council in the summer of 1972.

118. By contrast, Momoi, citing the higher importance of effective antisubmarine warfare sea forces and a competent radar early-warning network, does not believe that nuclear warheads add much to the country's tactical defense capabilities: "Japan's Defense Policies," pp. 110–11.

tion to oppose any emergency U.S. deployment of tactical nuclear weapons for the defense of Japan.[119]

The second question arose in August 1974, when—on the basis of statements by a member of the crew of the U.S. aircraft carrier *Midway*—the opposition charged that the ship had nuclear weapons aboard it when it entered a Japanese port. Testimony shortly thereafter by retired Rear Admiral Gene La Rocque before a subcommittee of the Joint Congressional Committee on Atomic Energy that U.S. ships capable of carrying nuclear weapons normally kept them aboard when they entered foreign ports added weight to these charges.[120] There were also allegations of a secret agreement between Japan and the United States permitting the transit of nuclear weapons through Japan, but the existence of such an agreement was denied by the Japanese government.[121]

The debate on this issue was carried prominently by the Japanese press. The U.S. government took its standard position, that it could not confirm or deny the presence of nuclear weapons, but it added that it had kept its commitment to prior consultation with the Japanese government. The Japanese government repeated its position that nuclear weapons could not be brought into Japan without prior consultation and said that the U.S. government had not requested consultation. Premier Tanaka told correspondents that he was convinced that nuclear weapons had not been brought in.[122] The Japanese press and public, however, found official assertions unconvincing.[123] Strong suspicions were expressed that the U.S. government interpreted its commitment to prior consultation as not applying to nuclear weapons temporarily brought into Japanese ports aboard

119. The firmness of this "third no" has been considered somewhat problematic. Hisashi Maeda notes the government's equivocal response to an inquiry by the UN secretary-general in January 1972 regarding the refusal of nonnuclear nations to receive nuclear weapons. The Japanese position was that this "should be taken up as part of our overall disarmament plan including international supervision": "Toward a Non-Nuclear Northeast Asia," *Japan Interpreter,* vol. 8 (Winter 1973), p. 23.

120. *New York Times,* October 8, 1974.

121. *New York Times,* October 15 and 17, 1974.

122. *Washington Post,* October 23, 1974.

123. In a *Sankei* public opinion poll published October 11, 45 percent of the respondents stated they thought that the United States had brought nuclear weapons into Japan in the past and 41 percent thought that the United States might have brought them in. Only 4 percent thought that they had not been brought in. Some 75 percent of the respondents in an *Asahi* poll said they were not convinced by Japanese government assurances that nuclear weapons had not been brought in; only 9 percent said they were satisfied with the government's explanations. No later polls are available, but they probably would show little change, for the Japanese press continued to express great skepticism about the Japanese government's position.

ships. The furor over the issue eventually died down, though it could readily be revived. Still, it did die down with surprising speed, perhaps because the Japanese public is more prepared to tolerate such practices, in support of deterrence, than has generally been assumed.

Problems of Coordination

Under the 1960 pact, the United States and Japan are to consult in case of threats to the security of Japan or to the international peace and security of the Far East. Beyond this commitment to meet in time of emergency, the two powers have sought to develop consultative machinery so as to conduct their defense activities more effectively in normal times. They have set up useful machinery, but there have been more complaints than sounds of satisfaction from both sides.

Impediments to Closer Cooperation

At issue are the consultative institutions themselves, the level of coordination, the failure to cover important problems, and inadequate steps to define and integrate defense burdens.

COORDINATING BODIES AND FUNCTIONS. The highest consultative body is the Security Consultative Committee (SCC), on which the United States is represented by the ambassador to Japan and the commander in chief, Pacific (CINCPAC), and Japan by the foreign minister and the head of the Defense Agency. Recognizing that the SCC meetings were too infrequent and formal, the two parties agreed in 1967 to establish a Security Sub-Committee (SSC) under the U.S. ambassador and Japan's vice-minister of foreign affairs.[124] This body has met more frequently, with informal sessions of useful give-and-take. To strengthen the apparatus further, another subcommittee was established early in 1973 to deal with base operations in Japan—in partial fulfillment of the Fukuda pledge to improve the working of the arrangements for prior consultation.[125] Japanese officials involved in its activities have found early performance of this second subcommittee to be quite satisfactory. It includes civilian and military officials from both sides, thus marking the first instance in which Japanese military officers have had representation on a bilateral security body.

124. Hearings, p. 1416.
125. *New York Times,* January 24, 1973.

This tardy appointment of Japanese military personnel to consultative bodies reflects another problem, the low rank and status held by uniformed officers in the Tokyo government.[126] The Japan Defense Agency itself has been thoroughly dominated by civilians, many of them on loan from other ministries whose interests they continued to represent during this temporary assignment. In addition, the individual services have operated on their own in projecting buildup plans and in developing their defensive missions.[127] National defense policy consequently has lacked an integrated focus, a handicap compounded by the gap between assigned tasks—particularly air defense, antisubmarine warfare, and the ground force's capacity to resist an invasion for a month—and the inadequate strength available for the mission. This has led to improvisations that related only partially to the formal mission and thereby reduced the coherence of national planning still further. Given these circumstances, it is not surprising that Japanese planning occurs without consultation or coordination with the United States. Nor is there an agreed-upon strategic perspective that both the United States and Japan can use as a common point of departure.[128]

POLICY ISSUES AND ADJUSTMENT. A related difficulty in systematic coordination arises from the government's desire to avoid giving prominence to military affairs. Because U.S.-Japanese security coordination is a political liability, the government has sought consistently to play down these talks, to give them a minimum of publicity. When the SSC became the forum at which truly substantive talks occurred, for example, the government first tried to keep this fact secret and then called the sessions merely "discussions."

More fundamentally, Japan is not prepared to make the basic adjustments in defense policy required for meaningful talks about a unified strategic outlook, defense plans, and allocation of missions. Such consultation would require consideration of security problems outside Japan,

126. Some of these problems are discussed in Emmerson, *Arms,* pp. 124–27.

127. The Fourth Five-Year Defense Plan (Japanese fiscal years 1972–76) recognized this defect and has as one of its objectives "increasing the effectiveness of the co-ordinated operations of the Three Services by encouraging harmonious co-operation among the Ground, Maritime and Air Self-Defense Forces." For text, see Japan Defense Agency, "Japan's Fourth Five-Year Defense Plan," *Survival,* vol. 15 (July–August 1973), pp. 184–87.

128. Shinohara notes that it has never been made clear how the execution of Japan's defense tasks "affects the division of responsibilities between Japan and the U.S.A. or the respective defense planning of the land, sea or air defense forces": "National Defense," p. 157.

the pinpointing of specific threats, and a following of the U.S. lead in devising operational plans. Japan thus could become entangled, even if indirectly, in military problems beyond its frontiers, and the United States would gain leverage to press Tokyo for forces required to carry out assigned missions.

On the benefit side, the Japanese would gain insight into U.S. defense plans and intentions, about which they are currently in the dark. They also would be able to probe into the level of support available from the United States in a crisis and measure this against the gap that exists between the responsibilities and the capabilities of the Self-Defense Forces —two examples of which are the availability of U.S. stocks in Japan for the undersupplied Ground Self-Defense Force and access to the U.S. air early-warning system.

Both considerations, however, pose several difficulties for the United States. The first involves the danger of leaks: the Japanese government has been notoriously unable to keep sensitive information out of the public domain. High LDP leaders, especially those of cabinet rank, repeatedly have resorted to revelations to advance their political positions.

A second concern is the prospect of Japan's coming quickly to depend on the United States to bear a larger share of Japan's own defense burden than the United States wishes to, whether protection of the sea lanes or air defense, on the grounds that the mission otherwise could not be carried out. American desires to keep Japan's responsibilities sharply defined—to induce Tokyo gradually to reach authorized force levels and to provide the forces with adequate logistical support—would be markedly impeded if lines of responsibility became blurred.[129] Such close linkage also could spur Japanese efforts to inhibit or prevent the United States from using the bases to respond to threats elsewhere in the Far East. Tokyo might argue that such actions would disrupt joint defense plans or could involve Japanese forces in unconstitutional activity abroad.

Finally, such ties would tempt LDP leaders to blame the United States for pressuring them into adopting unpopular defense measures as the price for joint defensive operations. Given the nature of Japanese politics, the use of such a deflector of responsibility would be difficult to

129. Drew Middleton cites U.S. civilian and military officials as urging Japan to a stronger defense effort, especially in protecting its sea lanes: *New York Times,* November 25, 1973.

resist, especially if the government actually wished to adopt such measures in the first place.

Bilateral Attitudes and Prospects for Change

Military cooperation today exists only at a primitive level. Japan is to protect its maritime lanes and the waters up to about 500 miles out to sea, an obligation derived from a little-noticed decision of the Japan Defense Agency reached early in the 1970s that extends Japan's admittedly still limited defense perimeter considerably. Japan also is supposed to meet all assaults below the level of a large-scale conventional attack and to maintain the capability of fighting against any invader for thirty days.[130] Thus, responsibility is divided according to territorial range and levels of combat intensity. But the two nations have not coordinated their plans, let alone devised a joint endeavor or logistical support. All that exists is a bare-bones annual contingency plan, developed by the headquarters of U.S. forces in Japan and the Japan Defense Agency, of how to respond to an attack.

Routine military cooperation exists only at the modest level of representation at one another's headquarters, exchanges of intelligence (especially about Soviet air and naval movements near Japan) and U.S. use of Japanese air defense facilities. In exercises, U.S. naval forces help Japan train in antisubmarine warfare and air defense, but there is no cooperation in Japan's actual coastal defense efforts. Under an agreement reached in the mid-1950s, the two air forces operate separately, and only Japanese planes scramble during defense alerts.[131]

Despite resistance to certain kinds of coordination, the Japanese government keenly feels the inadequacies inherent in present arrangements. The new subcommittee on bases gives Japan a better capacity to monitor U.S. activities at these installations but leaves many other problems unresolved. The Japanese are especially sensitive to their inadequacy at sea, even under normal conditions. With their zone of responsibility now extended to Okinawa, they are particularly anxious to develop greater coordination at sea. A suggestion of one LDP legislator is the creation by Japan, in cooperation with the United States, of a large sonar net cov-

130. Momoi discusses Japan's limited defense perimeter in "Japan's Defense Policies," p. 105.

131. For a table of the record of scrambles through 1969, see JIIA, *White Papers of Japan,* p. 47.

ering the area south of the home islands.[132] The Japanese are interested also in the establishment of a joint central information-control center in the home islands to monitor maritime activities in these waters. But although they desire cooperation to the south, which already is Japan's responsibility, they seek to avoid involvement in northern waters, in which, they argue, the Russians are too powerful, and feel the zone should remain an American responsibility.[133]

The Japanese also express concern over the American failure to place such working operations on a basis of equality, as called for under Article IV, in that only Japan has cabinet-level representation on the SCC. U.S. cabinet officials, by contrast, attend high-level meetings with European allies and other Pacific treaty signatories. Beyond the question of prestige, this has the practical effect of limiting discussions to parochial matters because the U.S. delegates lack the authority to deal with such higher-level issues as consideration of a joint defense program. The Japanese also feel that this arrangement effectively blocks them from learning about U.S. defense plans for Japan and from evolving a working naval relation.[134] The absence of routine exchanges of views at high levels also inhibits the development of new concepts for sharing defense responsibilities. Concerned for about a decade, Japanese officials have recently been pressing to institutionalize meetings between the U.S. secretary of defense and the director of the Japan Defense Agency. An exchange of visits took place in 1970–71, during which this point was raised, but it has not been followed up since.[135]

INDIVIDUAL OBJECTIVES. Better coordination would improve Japan's

132. Interview with Kazuo Tanikawa on August 23, 1972.

133. Some of the diplomatic difficulty, caution, and concern felt by the Japanese in their dealings with the northern problems are evident in Shigeo Ōmori, "Japan's Northern Territories," *Japan Quarterly,* vol. 18 (January–March 1970), pp. 18–26, which makes a strong case for the Japanese claim. See also Elizabeth Pond, "Japan and Russia: The View from Tokyo," *Foreign Affairs,* vol. 52 (October 1973), pp. 151–52: Pond sees prospects for limited progress, with Soviet power posing a problem for Japan but one that is held in check by U.S. and Chinese policies. Hellmann also notes the bilateral tensions while stressing the diminished likelihood of military confrontation, but he concludes with the observation that the Soviets and Japan may become more involved in security issues as the U.S. involvement diminishes and as the Soviet presence increases: "Confrontation," pp. 165–68.

134. The chairman of the Council on National Security Problems, Tadao Kusumi, was particularly emphatic on these points regarding consultation: interview on August 30, 1972.

135. Defense Agency Director Nakasone pressed this point while in Washington: *New York Times,* September 11, 1970.

defense planning, encourage more realistic levels of preparation, and open the way for combined contingency plans in time of emergency. Although the formidable obstacles noted above will persist, progress may become easier toward the end of the 1970s, when Japan's actual forces under arms come close to meeting requirements in terms of supply, equipment, and perhaps manpower.[136] Japanese defense officials and experts identify strategic concepts, staff consultations, and logistics and combat support planning as the most likely areas of cooperation. Informal staff talks and consideration of such specific problems as supply could provide useful points of departure. In addition, the type of structured and open consultations now held by the SSC could become more effective with a joint civilian secretariat and a small military staff to provide the SSC with agendas, estimates of specific situations, and analyses of territorial and functional problems that are of immediate concern. But the sensitivities of both parties—which wish to avoid either restraints (the United States) or entanglements (Japan) that could follow from such joint arrangements—will increase the difficulty of reaching agreements more directly related to such actual operations as force size, missions, deployments, and, above all, command.

The quest for autonomy, the domestic political difficulties attached to increased coordination, and the prickly issues of preparedness that the United States inevitably would raise restrain the Japanese from vigorously pursuing questions of coordination. For the United States, the need to maintain a maximum of freedom of activity, the determination to avoid involvement in those defense burdens which have been allocated to Japan, and the desire to keep as great a distance as possible from the rough and tumble of Japanese politics lead to a similar attitude. The negative consequences, however understandable, include inadequate Japanese strategic planning and the absence of a coherent combined defense posture—and, in general, the lack of substantial joint preparation to deal with a serious emergency.

136. Despite its strong bent toward autonomous defense, the 1970 White Paper also remains receptive to cooperative endeavors. The abstract states: "In this contemporary world, autonomous defense does not necessarily mean single-handed defense. If each nation enters into mutual co-operation with other nations while retaining its autonomy in order to protect its national interest, a collective security system thus formed is also one form of autonomous defense." JIIA, *White Papers of Japan,* p. 41.

CHAPTER FOUR

JAPAN'S DEFENSE EFFORT

Despite the problems that have arisen over the mutual security treaty and U.S. bases in Japan, the Japanese motivation to retain the security relation with the United States remains strong because Japan itself does not possess an armed force capable of defending Japan against large-scale attack and, for a variety of reasons, the Japanese people are not disposed to build such a force. Japan has chosen to keep its defense expenditures low relative to those of other major powers and to rely on the United States for advanced weapons, rather than to create a large defense production industry in Japan. The increase in defense expenditures, which roughly doubled in 1972–76 over the previous five-year period, has been criticized in Japan, both by those who consider it excessive and portending a return of militarism and by those who regard it as too little because it will not produce a force capable of repelling a large-scale conventional attack. Almost all shades of opinion oppose nuclear weapons for Japan, but there is marked reluctance nevertheless to ratify the nonproliferation treaty and thus close off that option.

U.S.-Japanese Cooperation

No strong differences of opinion have developed between the United States and Japan over the size and structure of the Japanese armed forces and the method of equipping them. The United States has tended to favor a quicker Japanese buildup, but in the absence of any serious outside challenge, the Japanese have chosen not to move more rapidly. The United States also has tended to prefer a larger proportion of military purchases from the United States than has occurred, but it recognizes that Japan is determined to increase the domestically built share of its armaments.

77

Compatible and Competing Interests

In the total context of bilateral security interests, Japan's defense effort is essentially compatible with U.S. objectives, and areas of concurrence considerably outweigh those of disagreement. The most important feature of the effort is the modest Japanese rearmament program, which has remained conventional and well below the upper ranges of this limited category. For example, Japan lacks a long-range air or naval capability, either for combat or transportation. Although it ranked twelfth internationally in military expenditures in 1970, about $1.5 billion, Japan stood at the bottom of a list of fifty-two states in proportional share of the budget, 7.2 percent.[1]

Japan also has responded to American urgings to bear a greater defense burden: by formally undertaking responsibility for conventional self-defense and over the years by rapidly raising the amounts devoted to defense.[2] These figures admittedly remain at relatively low and stable—even descending—levels as percentages of Japan's national budget and gross national product, at about 7 percent and 0.8 percent, respectively, in recent years. (Figures for 1958 were 11.1 percent and 1.26 percent, respectively; for 1964, 8.4 percent and 0.95 percent; and for 1969, 7.1 percent and 0.78 percent.)[3] But the startling growth in national wealth allowed a striking rise in the gross figure for defense expenditures: a fourfold increase between 1960 and 1970. The second defense buildup program (1962–66) totaled just under $4 billion; the third (1967–71), about

1. *United States Security Agreements and Commitments Abroad: Japan and Okinawa,* Hearings before the Subcommittee on U.S. Security Arrangements and Commitments Abroad of the Senate Committee on Foreign Relations, 91 Cong. 2 sess. (January 26–29, 1970), p. 1206 (hereafter referred to as Hearings). Senator Stuart Symington expressed dismay that Japan was spending $1.3 billion on defense in 1969, while the United States was spending in Japan alone almost half that total—$600 million—out of a total defense budget of about $80 billion.

2. As Under Secretary of State U. Alexis Johnson stated: "The primary responsibility for the defense of Japan, direct conventional defense . . . is entirely Japanese. We have no forces, either ground or air, in Japan that are directly related to direct conventional defense of Japan. This is entirely now a Japanese responsibility": ibid., p. 1167. Lieutenant General Thomas K. McGhee, USAF, added: "The air defense of Japan now is completely in the hands of the Japanese Air Self-Defense Force. We have no U.S. resources committed to this on a day-to-day basis": ibid., p. 1214.

3. International Institute for Strategic Studies, *The Military Balance, 1973–74* (London: IISS, 1973), p. 75.

$7.5 billion; and the fourth (1972–76) is projected at $16 billion.[4] Even this sizable increase during the 1970s will not bring expenditures up to the level of 1 percent of gross national product because of Japan's continuing rapid economic growth. Proposals to have the defense effort rise to 2 percent of GNP, which still would represent less than half the effort of the European democracies, have foundered on the judgment of the Liberal Democratic party leadership. Given the absence of a threat, the protective value of the mutual security treaty, and improvements in the Self-Defense Force through already-rising expenditures, LDP leaders believe it wiser to adhere to the present course.[5]

A third point of compatibility is Japan's continued willingness to rely on advanced American technology in such crucial fields as avionics, space, and nuclear energy. As a result, Japan really has not developed an independent military potential in the conventional realm, let alone the nuclear.[6] Moreover, the close tie between the two states in such advanced items as radar components, electronic countermeasures, and infrared seeker equipment improves collaboration in the fields of industrial engineering and manufacturing. This comes at a particularly propitious time, since military training programs for Japanese in the United States, which enabled future leaders to develop closer relations with their American counterparts, have been phased out because of their high cost and the elimination of U.S. military aid.

The problems are important though less significant than these points of compatibility. One difficulty, already noted, is Japan's inability to pro-

4. The earlier plans are summarized in capsule form by *Gekkan Ekonomisuto,* "The Evaluation of Japan's Defense Plans," *Japan Interpreter,* vol. 8 (Spring 1973), pp. 214–18. See also James H. Buck, "The Japanese Self-Defense Forces," *Asian Survey,* vol. 7 (September 1967), pp. 597–613.

5. For an early proposal to raise expenditures to 2 percent of the GNP, see Kiichi Saeki, "Collective Defense: A Realistic Guarantee of Japan's Security," *JSPIJ,* vol. 4 (April 1966), pp. 48–53. More recent discussions of what this would mean are in James H. Buck, "Japan's Defense Options for the 1970's," *Asian Survey,* vol. 10 (October 1970), pp. 891–93; and James W. Morley, "Economism and Balanced Defense," in Morley (ed.), *Forecast for Japan: Security in the 1970's* (Princeton University Press, 1972), pp. 14 and 25, in which he states that a 2 percent expenditure level would depress annual growth by only 0.5 percent. Japan Defense Agency (JDA), "The Defense of Japan" (October 1970; processed), appended chart 4, gives national defense expenditures of various nations as of 1970.

6. On the limited degree of actual autonomy enjoyed by Japan in the production of sophisticated equipment, see publication of Keidanren [Federation of Economic Organizations], "Our Views on the 4th Defense Building Program," August 12, 1970.

vide for its own conventional defense beyond a low level of threat. The United States may hold that conventional defense of Japan "is entirely now a Japanese responsibility,"[7] but this is not even remotely possible against a conventional Soviet attack or even a significant Soviet attack on Japan's air defense or sea lanes.[8] Japan could not retain supremacy in the air and command of the seas even around the home islands during the early stages of an air attack.[9]

A second point is Japan's total unwillingness to undertake defense obligations abroad, though this has not become an issue of contention. Formidable constitutional as well as domestic inhibitions exist, and the nearest concerned Asian state, South Korea, repeatedly has expressed fears of renewed Japanese domination. But whether Seoul would reject any Japanese involvement if assured of a continued U.S. presence is not certain. Clearly, however, near unanimity exists in Japan, among both supporters of the government and the opposition, that the country should avoid all foreign military entanglements and leave the burden of defending others to the United States. Although the United States recognizes and accepts Japan's self-limitation, it may adopt a less tolerant attitude by the end of the 1970s, especially if the trend toward détente in East Asia should falter.

Finally—and somewhat in contradiction to the foregoing—the United States has been somewhat unhappy over the degree of autonomy that Japan has sought in developing its own military production facilities. This desire has cost the United States considerable amounts in lost sales

7. Hearings, p. 1167.

8. In Japan Defense Agency, "Japan's Fourth Five-Year Defense Plan," *Survival*, vol. 15 (July–August 1973), pp. 184–87, it was stated that the fourth plan has a very limited objective: "dealing effectively with aggression on a scale not greater than a localized war in which conventional weapons are used" (p. 185); and that in case of invasion, "our country will counter indirect aggression and repel a small-scale direct aggression by our own efforts and, in case of an armed aggression *beyond such a scale,* we will *counter it with the cooperation of the United States.*" Emphasis added. For criticism of even this preparation for local, limited wars and indirect aggression as "lacking in factual content," see Hiroshi Shinohara, "National Defense," *Japan Quarterly,* vol. 18 (April–June 1971), p. 157.

9. See, for example, John Figgers, "The Outlook for Japan," *World Today,* vol. 27 (November 1971), p. 485; Ralph Clough, "East Asia," in Bruce Brown (ed.), *Asia and the Pacific in the 1970's* (Canberra: Australian National University Press, 1971), p. 16; and Buck, "Japan's Defense Options," pp. 897–99. On the other hand, Japan's regional security involvement is seen as a real possibility in Lawrence Olson, *Japan in Postwar Asia* (Praeger, 1970), pp. 238–42, and Donald C. Hellmann, *Japan and East Asia: The New International Order* (Praeger, 1973), pp. 168–93.

and, consequently, in the balance of payments. It also has impaired that standardization of equipment which can facilitate combined operations, particularly in time of emergency. Despite the additional cost, the Japanese government has sought an independent manufacturing capacity to preserve an option whereby it could provide expeditiously for its own defense should the need arise. Japan therefore has developed a small, elite, well-armed force instead of a larger but less well-trained and well-equipped combat establishment with greater reserves and stockpiles to meet an invasion.[10] Since no actual threat is expected to materialize in the next five years, at least, this approach has considerable merit. Thus, the United States is caught between conflicting desires: to have Japan shoulder its share of the burden as an equal and at the same time to remain sufficiently subordinate militarily so that it cannot strike out on an independent course or become a menace to other Asian states.

Increased Japanese Self-Sufficiency

The first step toward self-sufficiency centered on items requiring a minimum of technological sophistication, particularly for the ground forces: rifles, machine guns, self-propelled guns, armored personnel carriers, tanks, and the like. Japanese production in recent years has increased, mainly for air and naval forces, but with some advanced army equipment such as helicopters. At sea, it produces destroyers and destroyer escorts, minesweepers and related equipment, and submarines. In aircraft, it has produced a jet trainer, which will lead to a ground-support plane. It is developing its own fighter plane to supplement or replace obsolescent American equipment, as well as a transport aircraft.[11] The Japan Defense Agency also sought a new patrol plane and an airborne early-warning system, but cuts in the JDA budget proposals for the fourth plan have moved these more expensive items back to the waiting list. By 1980, Japan should be able to produce its own ground-to-air missiles, somewhere between the low Hawk and high Nike ranges. Conceivably, it could develop a fuel-cell submarine as a modest, less expensive substitute for the nuclear submarine; but it has decided not to produce a first-line airplane like the F-4 Phantom jet completely on its own, choosing to rely instead on the United States to provide such key tech-

10. For details of equipment produced in Japan, see *Gekkan Ekonomisuto,* "Evaluation," pp. 214–17; and JDA, "Japan's Fourth Five-Year Defense Plan," pp. 184–87.

11. The summaries in footnote 10 list specific equipment programs in detail.

nology as engines and avionics—though the United States will no longer produce the entire plane for Japan.[12] Ballistic missiles and nuclear-powered submarines, even in terms merely of developing a capability, lie in the more distant future.

Japan, therefore, does not expect to become a major military power by 1980. Though it will be edging closer to that potential, only a great shift in emphasis will enable it to jump from a highly skilled second-line position to that of a major independent power state.[13] Japanese defense production occupies only 0.4 percent of the country's total industrial capacity, and present plans augur little change.[14] The desire to produce more modern aircraft, submarines, larger surface vessels, and air-defense missiles, however, will grow and cannot be denied. At issue is whether the United States will continue to work with Japan in these and related fields to increase Japan's capacity moderately and, at the same time, to retain both some control through leasing and other techniques of cooperative production and a capability to discourage steps toward more advanced, politically sensitive weapons—in the long-range conventional as well as nuclear categories.

U.S.-Japanese Collaboration in Military Production

Collaboration between the United States and Japan in military production and equipment thus is a critical consideration. This has evolved from a system of grants-in-aid in 1950–65 totaling $854.3 million into one that combines sales, manufacturing in Japan under U.S. license (such as the F-104 and Nike ground-to-air missiles), and joint ventures of coproduction on a commercial basis; the last is based on an intergovernmental memorandum of understanding that allows the armed services and private corporations to work closely together.[15] The authority for many arrangements derives from the Mutual Defense Assistance Agreement of 1954, which remains an important basis for defense cooperation. In this

12. Regarding production of the Phantoms, see Makoto Momoi, "Japan's Defense Policies in the 1970's," in J. A. A. Stockwin (ed.), *Japan and Australia in the Seventies* (Sydney: Angus and Robertson, 1972), p. 114. Japan will produce 128 F-4EJ Phantom interceptors with equipment and material imported from the United States: *New York Times,* November 22, 1972.

13. Shinohara projects Japan's likely defense posture by 1976 and 1980, assuming a continued development along existing lines for the rest of this decade: "National Defense," pp. 156–58.

14. Ibid., p. 160.

15. Hearings, p. 1417.

connection the Military Assistance Advisory Group, which existed under that arrangement, was changed in 1969 to the Military Development Agency (MDA), composed of U.S. officials whose major function is the sale of hardware to Japan.

Illustrating the value of technical cooperation as a binding force, this small MDA, with a staff of ten, is deeply involved in monitoring and smoothing the collaboration between the Japanese and American firms engaged in coproduction programs such as that for the F-4 Phantom. This arrangement enables the United States to coordinate technical modifications in existing programs, as requested by Japan, and at the same time to stay informed about specific changes the Japanese make in American models.[16] Still, friction is bound to occur in the working out of guidelines under which the United States will be sufficiently responsive to Japanese desires to advance their technological base while also holding back sensitive or profitable technology during joint production ventures.

Japan's Conventional Forces

The size of the Self-Defense Force (SDF) has led to differences of opinion in Japan. Just as the United States has ambiguous attitudes about Japanese strength, so some arguments have developed in Japan for a still stronger force, in contrast to others holding that the military already shows signs of runaway growth. By any comparative standards, the force is modest in size; although on completion of the fourth buildup plan in 1976 it will jump from twelfth to seventh rank in the world, it will remain well behind the two superpowers, mainland China, West Germany, France, and the United Kingdom.

Buildup of the Self-Defense Force

Toward the end of the third buildup plan in November 1970, the authorized size of the Japanese defense forces was 240,000, of whom 180,000 were authorized in the Ground Self-Defense Force (GSDF); its actual strength at that time, however, was only 156,000, organized into five armies comprising thirteen divisions. The Maritime Self-Defense

16. For example, Japan will not manufacture its own advanced reconnaissance plane as yet. Instead it will produce fourteen RF-4E Phantom reconnaissance planes by March 1977: *New York Times,* November 22, 1972.

Force (MSDF) had 210 ships centering on 40 escort vessels (up to destroyer size) and 13 submarines, a total of 140,000 tons. It also had 200 aircraft. The Air Self-Defense Force (ASDF) had 925 fixed-wing aircraft organized into fourteen squadrons, whose mainstays were 192 of the F-104Js and 287 of the obsolescent F-86Fs. Air defense strength rested on five battalions of Hawk and four battalions of Nike surface-to-air missiles, and a computerized central air defense network. All forces combined had about 320 helicopters, of which 220 belonged to the GSDF.[17]

THE FOURTH DEFENSE PLAN. Under the fourth defense buildup plan (1972–76), the ground force will retain the same size and structure, with one additional infantry brigade on Okinawa.[18] Emphasis is on increased firepower and mobility, with Japanese-made tanks, armored personnel carriers, and helicopters replacing obsolescent U.S. models. A mechanized force of four armored divisions is being organized in Hokkaido. The ground-to-air Hawk battalions will rise from five to eight, with one stationed in Okinawa. The MSDF will grow by 100,000 tons, to 240,000, with naval construction at about the same pace as in the third plan: fifteen destroyers and destroyer escorts, five submarines, and other smaller vessels. Emphasis is on antisubmarine warfare and minesweeping capabilities. The MSDF also will acquire more aircraft for antisubmarine warfare and fleet air defense, modestly extend its area of patrol activities, improve command and control facilities, and develop defensive tactics against hostile landings.

Finally, the ASDF will retain about the same number of planes as before, but they will be upgraded in quality as the F-86s are phased out and 156 new F-4E Phantoms are brought on line, together with the new Japanese-designed fighter. Trainer and transport aircraft of domestic design also will replace obsolescent equipment.[19] The Nike antiaircraft battalions will increase from four to six, and in all, Japan will have one of the densest antiaircraft missile defenses in the world.

According to the fourth defense plan, by 1976 the GSDF is to have

17. Figures on the SDF are available in Shinohara, "National Defense," p. 157, which contains a table of forces as of November 1970; JDA, "Defense of Japan," appended chart 7: "State of Consolidation of Defense Power"; and Hearings, p. 1417. Osamu Kaihara noted that the MSDF was only one-tenth the size of the old imperial navy of 1941: "Real Character of the U.S.-Japan Security Treaty as Is Seen in the Fourth Defense Power Consolidation Plan," *Asia* (May 1972).

18. For a table comparing major items of equipment at the end of the third plan and as projected for the end of the fourth plan, see JDA, "Japan's Fourth Five-Year Defense Plan," p. 187.

19. Ibid., and Hearings, pp. 1213–14.

about 75 percent of the capability required for its projected defensive missions against conventional attack; but in contrast, the MSDF will be in the 50 percent range and the ASDF only slightly better.[20] It is estimated that by 1980, Japan will still have a GSDF of 180,000, but an air force of 1,000 modern planes and a navy of 300,000 tons.[21] The impact of the energy crisis and inflation led at the end of 1973 to a more austere defense budget than had been planned: $6.1 billion, up 19.7 percent but below the originally projected rise of 23 percent. As a result, the JDA received $3.9 billion for 1974–75, up 18 percent to a new high but still below the requested level. This led to a lowering of goals in strengthening the MSDF and the ASDF and required cancellation of orders for jets and tanks.[22] Consequently, the time frame of the fourth plan may be extended, and the plan may fail to attain its targets by 1976.

CURRENT LIMITATIONS AND PROJECTIONS FOR 1977–81. Despite these improvements, the SDF remains handicapped by its limited size and an inadequate logistical backup in relation to assigned missions in the home islands and Okinawa.[23] For example, the Soviet Far Eastern navy has a force of 900,000 tons, including 7 cruisers, 50 destroyers, and 110 submarines. With its modest-size combat and auxiliary ships, the MSDF has little capacity for extensive patrols, antisubmarine warfare, or coastal defense. It has difficulty even tracking Soviet movements through the narrow straits between Honshu and Hokkaido and cannot monitor the three main straits used by the Soviet fleet to enter Pacific Ocean waters. Japan remains highly vulnerable to mining and to a submarine blockade.[24]

Although air defense is completely a Japanese responsibility, the system remains relatively porous, vulnerable to undetected low-level approaches and to suppression of both its radar and communications facili-

---

20. These estimates, derived from the JDA, "Defense of Japan," are cited in Shinohara, "National Defense," p. 158.

21. JDA, "Defense of Japan."

22. These cuts occurred even though, under the reversion treaty, Japan is now responsible for the defense of Okinawa, and the fourth plan states this as one of its objectives: JDA, "Japan's Fourth Five-Year Defense Plan," p. 185. Japan has authorized an increase in air and naval forces by a few thousand each—to 45,067 and 42,347, respectively—and has placed an air wing on Okinawa. *New York Times,* September 24, 1973.

23. *New York Times,* December 23, 1973.

24. Osamu Kaihara emphasizes Japan's extensive vulnerability in all aspects of defense: "Real Character of the U.S.-Japanese Security Treaty."

ties.[25] It lacks reconnaissance aircraft and is weak in many defensive combat-related categories such as all-weather interceptors, air-ground support, and an air-to-ship attack capability. The defenders would have to destroy about 15 percent of all attacking aircraft, and it is doubtful whether even the projected ASDF will be up to such a task.

The ground forces remain too small and have an inadequate logistical system to handle their mission. The GSDF would have to triple in size to reach the strength required to defend the home islands against a landing attack should this unlikely prospect ever materialize. For example, it has been estimated by Defense Agency officials that if Hokkaido actually were invaded, Japan would need twelve divisions there to meet the challenge. The country also would have to improve a woefully inadequate system for delivering petroleum products and other military supplies, especially between islands, as well as provide six months' supplies to enable the GSDF to face an actual threat.

By means of the fifth plan (1977–81), assuming that it follows the incremental course of its predecessors, many components of the SDF will acquire essential defensive equipment and approach the levels required to cope with their missions. Many Japanese scholars and officials defend this moderate and gradual defense buildup.[26] The government gets around the constitutional prohibition against "war potential" by defining the notion as that capacity exceeding the minimum needed for national self-defense.[27] Although popular opinion did not support rearmament during the 1950s and 1960s, the government achieved its modest objectives through partial and cumulative buildup programs. Arguments in the 1960s favoring Japan's modest defense force ranged from the need to carry the country's share of the mutual defense burden to the claim that an unarmed Japan might tempt the communist countries and so precipitate a confrontation among the great powers that would endanger Japan. Acknowledging that a strong defense force also would be protecting U.S. bases, one observer argued that this benefited all Japan's neighbors and so improved the region's political stability.[28]

25. Hearings, pp. 1213–14, and interviews.

26. See, for example, Saeki, "Collective Defense."

27. For Japanese government arguments on how the no-war clause did not prohibit Japan's efforts at self-defense, see John K. Emmerson, *Arms, Yen and Power: The Japanese Dilemma* (Dunellen, 1972), pp. 52–53.

28. Yōnosuke Nagai, "Mao Tse-tung's Challenge to the American View of War," *Journal of Social and Political Ideas of Japan* (hereafter *JSPIJ*), vol. 4 (December 1966), pp. 90–91.

Japanese Attitudes toward Military Growth

Today, with emphasis on autonomous defense, the increasingly strengthened SDF is and probably will remain more widely accepted—provided, first, that it remains completely defensive and committed only to the homeland, and, second, that expenditures remain approximately at their current low proportion of gross national product. The public also accepts the policy, stated in the White Paper of October 1970, of stressing modernization and development rather than of making existing forces combat ready in the absence of an emergency.[29] The stand against developing offensive conventional weapons, as well as a nuclear force, also is supported by some defense experts, who reason that a Japan already determined not to become a nuclear power in any event would find long-range conventional weapons useless against a nuclear power in time of combat. They reject the argument that a Japanese effort in combined operations of this sort with the United States (whose involvement admittedly sustains the nuclear guarantee) would help significantly to deter or repel a large-scale conventional attack.

Some scholars who see no danger of a major foreign or internal threat are willing nonetheless to accept the SDF. They recognize that many people are worried about the country's safety and believe that a sovereign state should be able to defend itself with at least a moderate-size force. They also agree with the government's decision not to try to prepare for all eventualities. Some do not concur that the SDF needs the additional strength projected for the 1970s; others argue that the buildup plans must proceed because the SDF still is incapable of autonomous defense, whereas the Japanese population wishes to reduce its dependence on the United States. But almost all analysts recognize that autonomy cannot be achieved fully or the dependence eliminated because the country remains both so vulnerable to air attack along its long north-south axis and so dependent on imports for survival.[30]

29. In a poll by the prime minister's office in September 1969, 75 percent answered affirmatively to whether "it is good for us to have Self-Defense Forces." About 60 percent believed that Japan should fight if invaded, with 17 percent negative and 22 percent not knowing. The *Yomiuri* poll of June 1969 found more than 31 percent favoring a stronger SDF and more than 32 percent wishing to keep it at its present size.

30. Junnosuke Kishida stressed these points in discussing Japan's vulnerability in an interview on August 21, 1972. See also his "Non-Nuclear Japan: Her National Security and Role for Peace in Asia" (paper prepared for Peace in Asia conference, Kyoto, Japan, June 1972; processed).

PROJECTED ROLE OF THE UNITED STATES. Therefore, reliance on the United States will continue to rest not only on the nuclear guarantee but also on Japan's inability to project an adequate defense posture over the next decade.[31] At best, by 1981 it might be able to cope with a large-scale conventional attack for a month, its present mission, as against the seven to ten days of actual capability currently projected. Even this present projection would depend on rapid deployment of U.S. forces. For most of the coming decade, because of stockpile weaknesses, the SDF would need U.S. support after two months, even in a localized and limited emergency.

The Japanese also intend to proceed with coproduction endeavors and, where necessary, licensing programs in cooperation with the United States. Of the $16 billion allotted to the fourth plan before the 1973–74 energy crisis, approximately 30 percent, or $4.8 billion, was for major military hardware. (Another 10 percent also was allocated to smaller hardware items and maintenance costs.) Of this, Japan expected to produce 80 percent itself and import the remainder, some $960 million in major items (or somewhat over $1 billion all told). The United States was to provide the majority of these purchases, around $675 million to $700 million over the five-year period 1972–76. Because expenditures were to rise annually during the plan, the total 1976 defense budget was estimated at $4 billion, with $240 million of the $1.2 billion allocated for major hardware to be spent abroad. Japan also expected to make emergency imports, such as Tartar missiles, from the United States, both to relieve American balance-of-payments problems and for stockpiling purposes. The Japanese government planned to create a special foreign exchange account to receive JDA payments for these transactions from its annual budget. But its own balance-of-payments difficulties and growing inflation, stemming in part from the high price of energy, may lead Japan to reduce its special purchases from the United States, as well as slow down its fourth plan. Nevertheless, the current buildup program will remain above the level of the third plan and probably still will include acquisitions from the United States for stockpiling purposes, especially if Japan's balance of trade remains favorable.

Thus, Japan will continue to rely on the United States, through both one-time purchases and a gradual long-term increase in military imports, though the pace may be slower than originally anticipated. This reflects

31. Momoi stresses some of these issues in discussing Japan's very limited defense perimeter: "Japan's Defense Policies," p. 115.

a decision to have a limited indigenous military industrial capacity, one that will not seriously disturb plans for the civilian sector of the economy. A total commitment to self-reliance, though it might prove economically worthwhile in the long run, would be disruptive and expensive over the short haul.[32] Therefore, acquisition from the United States will continue in the fifth plan through purchases, licensing fees, and coproduction, with emphasis on adapting items to Japanese requirements. (For example, the F-4 Phantom jet has been modified in coproduction to provide the greater maneuverability sought by Japan.)

DIRECTION AND SHAPE OF MILITARY GROWTH. Critics who favor an SDF stronger than the one projected in recent governmental plans have not advocated sweeping changes. Some, in both government and the private sector, praise the greater emphasis on research and development and call for even more support because the trend contributes to autonomous defense and provides spin-offs to civilian industry.[33] Others want greater emphasis on air and naval forces, since these components would remain inadequate even at double their projected strength. Those most anxious about control of the seas would give the navy top priority instead of placing it last and would focus military growth on a nonnuclear MSDF. But all advocates of a stronger force, both within and outside the government, accept the need to proceed cautiously and within a strictly defensive mode and to maintain close ties to the United States.

Japanese defense experts are divided also on the long-term future shape of the SDF. They recognize that the armed forces will improve over the years in antisubmarine warfare capabilities, in adding more improved fighters, and in equipping the GSDF with better tanks and helicopters. They also agree that this somewhat strengthened force will rest firmly on a more substantial base of domestic production. But the advocates of a stronger SDF view these developments as extremely limited, allowing no significant change in Japan's restricted conventional strength. Furthermore, JDA officials believe that neither industry as a whole nor the gov-

32. Momoi observes that the defense industry ranks thirty-third in Japan, behind the leather industry. He also notes that only 10 to 12 percent of defense expenditures will go into new hardware, as against 50 percent or so for salaries, 10 to 15 percent to replace obsolescent weapons, and 10 to 11 percent on research and development: ibid.

33. Research and development efforts are noted in *Gekkan Ekonomisuto*, "Evaluation," pp. 214–18; and in JDA, "Japan's Fourth Five-Year Defense Plan," pp. 185–86.

ernment desires a truly independent productive capacity.[34] Private companies do not wish to risk funds or tie up resources for long periods to design and produce military equipment, and the government repeatedly has demonstrated its aversion to having Japan adopt an independent course. In particular, it has consistently rejected proposals for long-term projects in selected important items that would deepen the nation's shallow base for defense production.[35] Japan is unlikely to change course in the future, provided that a potent combination of unfavorable developments—massive increases in the erosion of U.S. credibility, in Japanese nationalism and strength of the Japanese Communist party, and in regional tensions—does not materialize.

Considerable criticism emanates at the same time from the opposite perspective: that Japan's continuing rearmament, however incremental, revives old dangers of militarism and arouses antagonism abroad. These arguments were particularly telling during 1970–71, when Peking made Japanese militarism its main target of propaganda. China's recent willingness to accept a larger SDF—a part of its general reorientation of policy to concentrate on the Soviet threat—has reduced the foreign impact. Academic and journalistic opponents still hold, however, that Japan's programs are too ambitious and out of balance.[36] They cite American findings that Japan in the 1970s already was spending annually more per soldier than do NATO countries, $10,000 as against $8,000, and in 1976 will approach the U.S. figure of $20,000. They particularly resent the "LDP Hawk" and SDF view of the defense forces as being in the stage of infancy, with concomitant implications of almost unlimited

34. Although not advocating a greater buildup or calling for everything to be produced in Japan, Keidanren criticized the way in which the JDA's Research and Development Office was run. It proposed a new forum to consider the research and production problems involved in a more rational and economic manner: "Our Views," pp. 3–4.

35. Keidanren figures for 1969 indicated that defense production as a percentage of total production of that item was more than 99 in weapons and 58 in aircraft; percentages then fell to 2.5 in vessels and were less than 1 percent for everything else, including vehicles, electronics, and communications equipment. Some firms engaged in important defense production, such as Mitsubishi Heavy Industry, admittedly favor a greater independent capacity for Japan. But for the most part, industrial leaders are oriented toward the civilian sector and view a major change toward military self-sufficiency as disruptive. Interview with Defense Agency officials in August 1972.

36. Junnosuke Kishida, noting that Japan soon will rank seventh internationally in defense spending, argues that the Nixon doctrine has accelerated Japan's takeover of some U.S. military burdens: "Ideas on Disarmament," *Japan Quarterly*, vol. 19 (April–June 1972), p. 148.

growth. They resent the absence of a ceiling on defense expenditures and wish to abandon the incremental approach so as to control the rapidly growing defense budgets. Particular resentment is expressed against increasing expenditures for hardware: because SDF manpower has little prospect of growing, these critics point out, it will be unable to cope with its assignments no matter how modern its arms. Because the inability of the SDF to expand in size is due to the lack of public support, the opposition therefore concludes that increases announced for the fourth plan and projected for the fifth are foolish expenditures.[37]

Yet the present policy seems too strongly rooted to change quickly. Given the U.S. commitment and the general détente in Asia, given the Japanese desire to maintain an option for autonomy in defense, and given the support of the Japanese public for a degree of national strength, this compromise program seems likely to persist, even if it fails to provide an adequate defense. Japan is slowly extending its capacity for action: in numbers of patrol planes, longer-range fighters, defensive missiles, the F-4 (a bomber as well as an interceptor), and artillery that could employ nuclear ammunition. It could make strides toward autonomy over a five-year period if it so chose. But thus far it has allowed its ally to retain effective control over critical items that it produces itself, has avoided development of advanced conventional weapons, and has kept its forces at a minimal level.[38]

The two main issues concerning Japan's defense effort therefore are not currently operational. One would involve the question of whether to opt for a really autonomous defense, a choice that if made would signify a major change in the national mood, the situation in Asia, and the

37. The GSDF reserve did grow from 36,000 in the 1960s to 60,000 by 1971, but the regular ground force has not grown in recent years, and there are no plans to go above the 180,000 level in total authorized forces.

Concern in Japan over the absence of a maximum ceiling is noted in T. C. Rhee, "Japan: Security and Militarism," *World Today,* vol. 27 (September 1971), p. 399. The alleged excess of armaments in proportion to manpower was raised frequently by academic and journalist critics of the defense program during interviews in August and September 1972.

38. In fact, many Japanese argue that it is the United States that has been pushing Japan toward a greater defense effort, much against its own wishes. They add that they do not want to rearm beyond present and planned levels and resent U.S. pressures on this point. See Figgers, "The Outlook for Japan," p. 485. John K. Emmerson and Leonard A. Humphreys also conclude that Japan will not make a substantial change in its incremental approach to military technology and armed strength in the near future: *Will Japan Rearm?* (American Enterprise Institute for Public Policy Research, 1973), chap. 6.

nature of the American alliance.[39] At the other extreme is Japan's inability to cope with middle-range conventional military challenge. This would become a problem only in a sharply changed international context, one that would strain the alliance at one of its weak points, that of inadequate coordination.

The Nuclear Issue and the Nonproliferation Treaty

Japan's horrendous wartime experience, its constitutional restraints, and a deep popular opposition to militarism all sustain Japan's aversion to nuclear weapons—for anyone. Yet the revival of nationalism, the wish to keep all options open, the desire to avoid hindering development of nuclear power for peaceful purposes, and objections to a formally inferior status have led the government to move slowly in ratifying the nonproliferation treaty (NPT) and to keep open the possibility of acquiring defensive nuclear weapons.

Japanese Attitudes and Status

There is no doubt that the Japanese public as a whole opposes nuclear arms and the American deployment of such weapons on Japanese soil. Numerous and formidable legal restraints reflecting this attitude range from the prohibitions of Article IX of the constitution to the law on atomic energy by which the country has limited itself to peaceful purposes.[40] U.S. atomic energy legislation and the mutual security treaty,

39. The belief that rising economic power inevitably will bring on a resurgence of military might has enjoyed currency in recent years. Takuji Shimano argues vigorously that such fears are unfounded: "Economic Growth and the Rise of Militarism," *Japan Interpreter*, vol. 8 (Spring 1973), pp. 208ff. Hidejirō Kotani argues in the same vein, calling such reasoning simplistic and noting that it ignores political and social realities in Japan: "Views on the Resurgence of Militarism," *Japan Interpreter*, vol. 8 (Spring 1973), pp. 199–203. Morley calculates that real autonomy—that is, superpower status—would require annually up to 10 percent of an estimated GNP of over $450 billion in the mid- to late 1970s, an allocation to defense purposes which is economically possible but most unlikely to occur: "Economic and Balanced Defense," p. 11.

40. Emmerson, *Arms*, pp. 342–43. The *Yomiuri* poll of June 1969 asked whether Japan should possess nuclear weapons. Only about 16 percent responded yes as against about 72 percent who said no and 12 percent who did not know.

Japan's ratification of the limited test ban treaty, and its signing (but not yet ratifying) of the NPT provide additional international checks on a shift in policy. Any effort to change the policy would encounter fierce opposition in the Diet and would severely polarize national politics and public opinion. Moreover, the advent of military nuclear power would give real impetus to what is still a very small military-industrial complex and thereby substantiate fears of revived militarism.[41]

STRATEGIC CONSIDERATIONS. Defense analysts outside the government, including those who favor a stronger SDF, display a near consensus against nuclear armament. Among the many arguments they advance is the claim that nuclear weapons, which served as a basis of strength and then prestige in the two previous decades, are now of little military value in an age in which security must be found through diplomacy in the context of a multipolar setting.[42] Moreover, they add, although such weapons might well prevent a major war, they cannot prevent small conflicts, and any Japanese nuclear force would be too small for deterrence and irrelevant for local wars. As to possible Soviet and Chinese dangers, Japan could neither match the Soviets nor be capable of severely damaging a massive underdeveloped state such as China, whose population remains overwhelmingly rural and whose industrial strength is widely dispersed. One expert argues that even if Japan could develop a secure sea-based second-strike force—a doubtful proposition because this requires a widely dispersed base and communication system —it would not appear credible because the home islands are so vulnerable to destruction.[43]

A rearmament program aimed at developing a sufficiency against China runs the risk of significantly destabilizing an already uncertain Asian political setting.[44] It could easily rekindle animosities in Southeast Asia and lead to the political isolation of Japan—especially if Japan

41. Emmerson, *Arms*, pp. 354–57.

42. See, for example, Kishida, "Non-Nuclear Japan," p. 3.

43. Momoi stresses this aspect of the vulnerability of Japan's highly urbanized society: "Japan's Defense Policies," pp. 108–09.

44. On the other hand, the problem of meeting the challenge from China— in direct security terms or in the contest for prestige and influence in East and Southeast Asia—was treated a few years ago as one of the most likely reasons for Japan seriously to consider the acquisition of nuclear weapons. See, for example, Hellmann, *Japan and East Asia*, pp. 162–63; and Buck, "Japan's Defense Options," pp. 894–95. Olson saw the motivation in more general terms of security, prestige, technological development, and the emulation of others: *Japan in Postwar Asia*, p. 241.

were to produce nuclear weapons over American opposition. Such a step, of course, also could endanger the survival of the MST. In the mid-1960s, Japanese analysts recognized the contributions of nuclear weapons to China's power status, but they argued that, if a contest for influence developed between the two Asian states, the challenge could be met in the economic and cultural arena.[45] Security experts in the Liberal Democratic party recommended at that time that Japan develop nuclear and space technology for peaceful purposes in order to avoid a sense of inferiority relative to the communist powers.[46] The Japanese also rejected the Gaullist arguments of General Gallois at that time. In both his writings and in a visit to Japan, Gallois held that no country could depend on another for ultimate protection because the commitment endangered the protectors. The Japanese retorted that he was confusing the strategy of deterrence with actual war, that the two could be separated, and that the former would work.[47]

The nuclear ecology argument, which holds that only a state with considerable physical and economic proportions is suited to possess nuclear weapons, has been especially persuasive in Japan. Its smallness makes the weapon less valuable by preventing rational deployment and proportionately more expensive, since overall wealth is partially a function of geographical size. By this reasoning, France and Britain erred in developing the weapons, mainly because they did so before this argument became as self-evident as it now is.[48]

Japan has additional handicaps, not the least of which is its closeness to Soviet and Chinese soil. This factor exposes Japan's population and industrial centers to short-range assault, to which it would have to retaliate with numerous long-range missiles to reach equivalent targets in

45. See, for example, Masataka Kōsaka, "Japan as a Maritime Nation," *JSPIJ*, vol. 3 (August 1965), pp. 49–53.

46. This was the thrust of recommendations by Kei Wakaizumi in 1966: "Chinese Nuclear Armament and the Security of Japan," *JSPIJ*, vol. 4 (December 1966), pp. 72–79.

47. For a more recent restatement of Japanese opposition to the Gaullist argument, see Shinkichi Etō, "Japan and America in Asia during the Seventies," *Japan Interpreter*, vol. 7 (Summer–Autumn 1972), pp. 246–48.

48. Kishida has vigorously advocated this position: "Non-Nuclear Japan," p. 2; and in an interview on August 21, 1972. Kunio Muraoka argues against the feasibility of defending the heavily populated, vulnerable home islands with nuclear weapons: "Japanese Security and the United States," *Adelphi Papers*, no. 95 (London: International Institute for Strategic Studies, 1973), pp. 24–26.

the communist nations. Other difficulties include a shortage of good locations for production plants because of the scarcity of water and the danger of earthquakes.[49] In addition, Japan would have to renounce the limited test ban treaty in order to conduct the above-ground tests necessary for weapons development. If the decision were made to go ahead, several years would be needed to collect an ore stockpile and develop a uranium enrichment process, as well as to produce the necessary early-warning system and sophisticated computer technology.

MAINTENANCE OF OPTIONS. Yet the rejection of nuclear weapons has remained carefully qualified. When, in 1971, Foreign Minister Aiichi and Prime Minister Satō adopted the three nuclear principles—abjuring manufacture, possession, and introduction into Japan of nuclear weapons—they limited their commitment to the life of the Satō cabinet, though the prime minister was quoted as saying that Japan would disapprove of bringing in nuclear weapons "as long as an LDP Cabinet is in office."[50] The opposition Socialist party considered this a weak argument because for Japan to reject an ally's request under prior consultation while claiming protection under the U.S. nuclear umbrella made little sense. For his part, Prime Minister Satō refused to have his three principles formalized as a Diet resolution.[51]

Japanese governments also have been at pains to keep open a legal path to nuclear weapons, arguing since 1958 that defensive nuclear weapons were not unconstitutional. The white paper of 1970 reaffirmed this point more sharply by holding that small nuclear weapons that did not constitute an aggressive threat were legally and constitutionally permissible if needed for self-defense—while adding that Japan had no plans to develop such an arsenal.[52]

It has been noted by various observers that the famed nuclear allergy following World War II diminished as a new generation emerged. A large percentage of the public, although opposed to such weapons, ex-

---

49. Some of these difficulties are discussed in Momoi, "Japan's Defense Policies," p. 109.

50. Emmerson, *Arms,* p. 178.

51. Ibid., pp. 343–44.

52. The Japan Defense Agency has stated that "if small-size nuclear weapons are within the scale of real power needed for the minimum necessary limit for self-defense, and if they are such as will not be a threat of aggression toward other nations, it is possible to say that possession thereof is possible, in legal theory": "Defense of Japan," p. 20.

pected that they would be acquired in the future.[53] The 1970 white paper presentation reflects this tentative trend. Similarly, in 1972 a Japanese naval official discussed, without drawing criticism, the possibility of obtaining a nuclear-powered submarine; such action would have raised a furor in previous years. It has been observed that the small minority favoring acquisition of nuclear weapons might grow in the future if the international situation deteriorates, especially if the strategic arms limitations talks between the United States and the USSR should fail,[54] Japanese-Chinese relations should worsen, or the number of nuclear powers should expand.

In regard to an expanding number of nuclear powers, some observers felt that for India to go nuclear would have a strong psychological impact on Japan.[55] India's nuclear explosion of May 18, 1974, allegedly for peaceful purposes, did disturb Japan and other nuclear-capable powers considerably and led five days later to a Diet resolution criticizing the action. Foreign Minister Ohira's immediate reaction, however, was

53. Thus, the *Yomiuri* poll of June 1969 found 32 percent saying yes when asked whether Japan will possess nuclear weapons in ten years as against 36 percent saying no and 32 percent did not know. Etō, in "Japan and America," p. 246, noted the large number (about 72 percent) who were against acquiring nuclear weapons as evidence that this was unlikely to occur. By contrast, however, the number of those favoring Japan's possession of such weapons rose from 3 percent in 1954 to only 16 percent in 1969. Findings similar to these, but with a somewhat different emphasis, are described in Yasumasa Tanaka, "Japanese Attitudes toward Nuclear Arms," *Public Opinion Quarterly,* vol. 34 (Spring 1970), pp. 26–42. He viewed the Japanese as still not favoring nuclear tests and military power, though they seemed to consider these less undesirable in 1966 than in 1961. The younger people in particular were less inhibited on both counts; they considered these actions as undesirable but were willing to contemplate such acquisitions if necessary for survival.

54. Walter C. Clemens argued that round one of the strategic arms limitations talks was essential to maintaining the status quo in U.S.-Japanese relations and that a failure would drive Japan on an autonomous military course: "SALT, the NPT, and U.S.-Japanese Security Relations," *Asian Survey,* vol. 10 (December 1970), pp. 1042–43.

55. In contrast, George Quester estimated that the Japanese did not care about India as a precedent: "Japan and the Nuclear Non-Proliferation Treaty," *Asian Survey,* vol. 10 (September 1970), p. 775. Tanaka, however, believed that continued proliferation would have an impact on Japanese attitudes: "Japanese Attitudes," p. 42. In a comparative study, Wayne Wilcox estimated that the two countries face quite different situations, with Japan facing much less pressure to go nuclear because of its U.S. tie and the absence of any major confrontation with the communist powers: "Japanese and Indian National Security Strategies in the Asia of the 1970's: The Prospect for Nuclear Proliferation," *Adelphi Papers,* no. 92 (IISS, 1972), pp. 30–39.

to reassert Tokyo's determination to rely on the U.S. security tie for nuclear protection.[56]

Should regional nuclear confrontations, even outside East Asia, occur in the future, these might lead Japan to think seriously about nuclear arms. If such a deterioration in international affairs were to occur, causing the United States to disperse its power and divert its attention from Asia, Japan could come to view nuclear weapons as a prudent investment that would protect the country from involvement, through weakness, in dangerous confrontations.

U.S. ROLE. It has been estimated that if Japan were to follow the unlikely course of acquiring nuclear weapons, the alliance with the United States also might be terminated, thereby increasing the instability of an already fluid Asian situation. For the present, Japan remains committed to the status quo, though many observers expect it to develop the technology for producing weapons, but not to go beyond sophisticated, commercial-peaceful uses. This would satisfy current economic needs and provide the basis for a conversion to military production in the next decade should this prove necessary.

The role of the United States thus becomes doubly crucial: in maintaining a credible deterrent and in satisfying economic and psychological needs in the area of commercial use.[57] A high degree of responsiveness to peaceful use also would enable the United States to influence the evolution of Japan's nuclear technology. Equally important is a clear Japanese perspective on American desires and expectations. Despite official U.S. policy against proliferation, many Japanese gained the impression around 1970 that the United States expected—and would tolerate—Japanese nuclear armament.[58] Thus, attitudes of private American scholars and experts as well as government officials will have an important bearing on Japanese policy. For example, the negative American views expressed on this subject at a conference in Kyoto in 1972 had an impact. Of even greater importance would be a continuing inter-

---

56. Japan protested immediately: "The Government can only express regret because we have been and are still against any nuclear test by any nation for any reason": *New York Times*, May 19, 1974.

57. William R. Van Cleave and Harold W. Rood noted Japan's high dependence on foreign technology and fuel, with needs well above those of India: "A Technological Comparison of Two Nuclear Powers: India and Japan," *Asian Survey*, vol. 7 (July 1967), p. 485.

58. The writings of Herman Kahn and others left this impression; see his *The Emerging Japanese Superstate* (Prentice-Hall, 1970).

est by U.S. officials in joint commercial ventures to dissuade Japan from developing an independent capability in nuclear diffusion technology.

Nuclear Needs for Peaceful Development

Japan has a legitimate need for enriched uranium as nuclear fuel, an increasingly vital source of energy, in the near future. It is already planning to have the second-largest nuclear-power capacity in the world, after the United States, by 1980,[59] which it expects will satisfy one-quarter of its rapidly expanding needs. The United States is the only supplier of enriched uranium at present. Japan's requirements are growing fast, probably to quadruple during the 1970s, and the cautiousness of American responses to increased Japanese demand evokes concern in Tokyo over inadequate or curtailed deliveries in the future.[60] For example, existing arrangements specify a ceiling on quantity that can be raised only by joint agreement, which could lead to delays caused by internal American disagreements on how to expand its own uranium enrichment capacity. If the United States cannot be relied on to meet future needs, Japan may try to go it alone.[61] It already has had offers of enriched fuel from other nations and is prospecting on a considerable scale. It is expanding its research and development in this field and is determined, in any event, to produce about one-third of its own needs to reduce its dependence on others. With considerable sums invested in centrifuge, ion, and gaseous diffusion processes,[62] Japan will be able to go forward

59. Japanese aspirations are detailed in Japan Institute of International Affairs (hereafter JIAA), *White Papers of Japan,* and aim at 8,660 megawatts by 1975 and 27,020 by 1980. By the year 2000, Japan hopes to have 164,000 megawatts, with nuclear power providing 46 to 47 percent of its electricity: Van Cleave and Rood, "A Technological Comparison," pp. 487–88. By comparison, the United States aims at 1.2 million megawatts by 1980, with nuclear power producing 55.8 percent of the nation's electricity, compared with 4 percent in 1973: *New York Times,* March 8, 1973.

60. The Japan Atomic Energy Commission's long-range program estimates that the country will need 13,000 and 90,000 metric tons of natural uranium by 1975 and 1980, respectively: JIIA, *White Papers of Japan,* p. 20. Technical problems and environmental complications, however, may cause significant cutbacks in the plans of both states. In Japan, for example, the plan to go from six nuclear power plants today to sixty-six in 1985 may not be feasible: *New York Times,* February 6, 1974.

61. By April 1970 electric utilities had acquired 35,000 short tons of uranium through long-term purchase contracts. A bilateral U.S.-Japanese agreement on enriched uranium assured Japan of 161 tons of U-235: JIIA, *White Papers of Japan,* p. 20.

62. *New York Times,* February 6, 1974.

on its own if necessary, even though research expenditures are small compared to those of the United States; for example, in nucelar fusion only $3 million for 1974–75 compared to $100 million. It prefers American technology and is making its own reactors with American technology, but continuing difficulties with the United States could lead it to bilateral or multilateral ventures with other nations. These arrangements could enable Japan to develop an enrichment plant and to acquire fuel through sources not amenable to U.S. control.[63]

Although improved technology and the acquisition of plutonium from nuclear-power reactors increase Japan's ability to move toward nuclear weapons, it has not proceeded in this direction. Plutonium is produced in small amounts today as a fuel by-product, but U.S. and International Atomic Energy Agency (IAEA) safeguards and inspections accurately account for this material.[64] Japan has one other nuclear arrangement, with France, for chemical separation of nuclear fuel, but this is essentially to clean up fuel already produced for more efficient use in the reactors, not to add to the total.

The ultimate answer appears to be U.S.-Japanese cooperation on the fast-breeder reactor to provide power and at the same time increase the fuel supply.[65] Japan would like very much to develop this on its own, but the costs are staggering and massive technical problems are involved in reaching commercial feasibility. Because these difficulties confront the United States as well as Japan, a basis exists for a joint effort in this area over the next decade—which in turn would add an incentive for American cooperation in supplying enriched uranium to Japan in the interim years.

In space programs, the substantial amount of sophisticated and releasable technology has made U.S.-Japanese relations smoother. Of past

63. American recognition of this issue was reflected in the joint communiqué of the Tanaka-Nixon meeting in Washington on July 31 and August 1, 1973. It advocated cooperation to secure "a stable supply of enriched uranium, including cooperation in the necessary research and development" and a joint venture to that end. They agreed to foster a joint study of "the construction of a uranium enrichment plant in the United States in which Japan might participate": U.S. Department of State, "The United States and Japan: Prime Minister Tanaka's Visit, July 31–August 1, 1973," Publication 8740, East Asian and Pacific Affairs Series 210 (September 1973), p. 7.

64. For a thorough discussion of safeguards, see Ryūkichi Imai, "Nuclear Safeguards," *Adelphi Papers,* no. 86 (IISS, 1972); see also Hearings, pp. 1217–18.

65. Van Cleave and Rood discuss Japan's early interest in fast breeder reactors: "A Technological Comparison," p. 488.

agreements, the most important was the release of technology for the Thor-Delta, which is well suited for satellite launchings and yet does not possess military characteristics.[66] After first trying to develop a larger booster on its own, Japan has decided to use the Thor-Delta as the first stage in its current launcher program, which will save time and money and increase the payload. Japan will manufacture it through a licensing arrangement and produce the other two stages itself. By providing such support, the United States keeps close to Japan's evolving space technology and can guide Japan toward preferred lines of technical development such as liquid fuel, rather than the solid varieties that are more suitable for military purposes.[67]

But even in this relatively successful enterprise, the United States often has been slow to adjust to changing attitudes and new sets of requirements in Japan. Some delays or failures to be responsive are caused by desires of American producers to keep certain categories of advanced technology out of other hands as long as possible. Currently, for example, the Japanese want a payload above the 300 kilogram level and thus need modifications in the Thor-Delta booster. The issue then becomes American responsiveness. Sufficient American support would continue to direct Japan's interest away from a military missile program, enable the United States to stay knowledgeable about Japanese capabilities, and keep Japan dependent on U.S. technology.

Japanese Reservations about the Nonproliferation Treaty

In its final form, the nonproliferation treaty reflected a number of suggestions by Japan and other nonnuclear states.[68] It prohibited the receipt or production of nuclear weapons by nonnuclear states and required them to accept verifiable safeguards. But it also fostered the exchange of equipment and techniques for peaceful uses of nuclear energy and promised that the benefits from nuclear explosives would be made available at low cost. All signatories also undertook to pursue

66. For American labor's opposition to the transfer of this and related technology to Japan, see *New York Times,* March 7, 1973.

67. Japan's fifth space shot actually marked its first truly accurate satellite launch, done on February 17, 1974, with an MU-3C rocket. The cumulative cost for Japan's space program from the beginning to March 1974 had cost about $460 million. For one year 1974–75 alone, the pace has increased to almost $200 million, but much of this reflects inflation: *New York Times,* February 18, 1974.

68. Hearings, p. 1201.

nuclear and general disarmament. Finally, the treaty runs for twenty-five years, with review after five years, and includes the right of withdrawal. When Japan signed, it stressed that it would have to consider, before ratifying, whether France and China acceded or at least did not act contrary to NPT obligations. Tokyo also emphasized the need for progress toward nuclear disarmament, which it deemed essential for equality, and took note of the escape clause.[69]

At present, the question of ratifying the nonproliferation treaty has become a focal point of attention regarding Japanese self-restraint.[70] Japan has several objectives in its arms control policy, some of which are conflicting. It genuinely desires to have the nuclear arms race curtailed through self-limitations by the superpowers and accession to the NPT by the remaining key nonsignatory states. But the Japanese government also wants the United States to retain a credible deterrent in view of Soviet strength and China's refusal to accept arms control, and it has never made extensive self-limitation by the United States a condition for ratification of the NPT. The Japanese also desire political equality and find unpalatable a treaty that establishes two classes of states, with themselves the inferior of the two.[71] Finally, Japan fears a discrimination in the development of nuclear technology for peaceful purposes that would hamper its own development and keep it from competing successfully in the commercial uses of atomic energy, especially for its export market.

Japan's hesitance led it to delay signing the NPT of July 1968 until February 3, 1970. Opposition arguments included a reluctance to yield formally the right to make such weapons, with the concomitant inability to transfer the benefits from research on weapons technology to peaceful uses. In addition, fear of a loss of security was expressed and objections were raised that the treaty discriminated in favor of the nuclear powers. The U.S.-U.K.-Soviet promise of June 19, 1968, to act through the UN Security Council if any state became a victim of, or was threatened by, aggression involving nuclear weapons did not appear satisfactory.[72]

69. Emmerson, *Arms,* pp. 346–47.

70. Donald C. Hellmann holds that the United States is following a dubious policy in pressing Japan to ratify the NPT: "The Confrontation with *Realpolitik,*" in James W. Morley (ed.), *Forecast for Japan: Security in the 1970's* (Princeton University Press, 1972), p. 163.

71. For these reasons, Clemens holds that continued progress in the strategic arms limitation talks is closely related to Japan's attitude on the NPT, whose ratification he strongly favors: "SALT," p. 1043.

72. Emmerson, *Arms,* pp. 345–46.

Admittedly this pledge concerned states with whom the United States lacked security arrangements, and the mutual security treaty is a much more binding bilateral obligation. The effect of ratifying the NPT, however, would be to increase Japan's dependence on the MST.[73]

There is a general feeling in Japan today that the country should continue to proceed slowly in considering ratification. A main drawback is that the treaty closes off an option, though one unlikely to be exercised, which could become especially important should nonratification become a symbol of independence. Even the five-year review procedure and the right of renunciation do not mitigate NPT restrictions in Japanese eyes. Because any withdrawal would either create a great diplomatic disturbance or heighten an already critical situation, it would be a difficult step to take, especially with other states pressing Japan to stay its hand.

A second problem is that of U.S. credibility and the heavy reliance on the mutual security treaty that ratification signifies. The comparison with West Germany, which also has signed but not yet ratified the treaty, is considered inappropriate because Bonn enjoys a higher degree of security as part of a European defense system, whereas Japan has only the American tie. On the other hand, ratification probably would increase the U.S. sense of obligation to defend Japan against attack. But the increased atmosphere of détente may make the problem of U.S. reliability less pressing over the next few years and thus reduce opposition to ratification. And if ratification occurs as part of a general process of lessening tensions in Asia, it may appear less as a unilateral concession and so arouse less nationalist resentment.[74]

A third issue involves Japan's access to commercial use and related questions of inspection and equality of treatment with West Germany. The Japanese genuinely fear that IAEA inspection procedures will harm

73. Hearings, p. 1200.

74. Arguments for regional arms control are often made in this context. Those who wish Japan to follow a new course in security policy also stress this approach, usually in the form of a nuclear free zone embracing at a minimum the two Koreas and Japan. See, for example, Hisashi Maeda, who recognizes that this would represent a U.S. concession, but who feels that it is bearable because the U.S. deterrent in the area rests mainly on sea power: "Toward a Non-Nuclear Northeast Asia," *Japan Interpreter*, vol. 8 (Winter 1973), pp. 22–24. Junnosuke Kishida also advocates the nuclear free zone: "Japan's Non-Nuclear Policy," *Survival*, vol. 15 (January–February 1973), pp. 19–20. He also calls for the banning of all tests, stating that this would require a sacrifice by Peking, in contrast to nuclear free zones and no-first-use pledges, which are simply to China's benefit: "Ideas on Disarmament," pp. 150–52.

their nuclear energy program.[75] They express concern over industrial espionage by means of the inspection process, a matter of considerable importance to Japanese industry, which hopes to develop nuclear power plants and reactors for a lucrative export market. Admittedly, Japan has no laws against covert acquisition of technical knowledge in commercial or industrial pursuits, but it has a valid worry about legalizing such access for foreigners.

Underlying this concern is the country's experience with IAEA inspectors, who police the industry under Japan's arrangements with the United States, the United Kingdom, and Canada for purchase of nuclear materials. Not only has the agency's inspection process apparently been aimed disproportionately toward Japan—twenty-two of the first twenty-nine reactors examined were in Japan—but also techniques such as demands in 1970 for unannounced night visits to a reactor angered the Japanese because of the implication of untrustworthiness. Further, there is widespread determination to be placed on an equal footing with West Germany, which is to undergo inspection by the other member states of the European Community of Atomic Energy (EURATOM) rather than by the IAEA. Japan therefore insists on self-inspection or some other equivalent treatment; and at times it has demanded as well that it be required only to produce its records and not throw its facilities open to physical inspection.[76] After lengthy negotiations with the IAEA, however, these questions finally were resolved to the satisfaction of the Japanese government, and a safeguards agreement with the IAEA was initialed in February 1975.

Of less significance but also bothersome is the prohibition against nuclear explosions, since these have utility for nonmilitary purposes. Japan remains unsatisfied with merely the right to hire the knowledge. The government also wants to remove prohibitions on the transfer of certain types of peaceful application and related information, withheld because this knowledge could be adapted to the production of nuclear weapons.

It can be claimed that the independent peaceful uses argument is somewhat unreal because Japan is so closely tied to the United States, does not invest sufficient capital to go on its own course, and can pur-

75. For a discussion of new approaches and remaining problems of safeguards, see Imai, "Nuclear Safeguards," pp. 11–20.
76. For these and related questions, see Emmerson, *Arms*, pp. 348–49.

chase needed technology from the more advanced powers. Still, the wedding of economics to nationalism in this issue makes it mandatory that Japan receive some satisfaction regarding inspection procedures, equality of treatment, and access to peaceful technology. Although little public pressure exists for ratification, satisfaction on these counts and continued progress toward arms control in the strategic arms limitation talks will make Japan's accession to the NPT fairly likely.

CHAPTER FIVE

EASING THE STRESSES

The security policy of the United States toward Japan certainly must be meshed closely with both economic and diplomatic policy. Questions of trade relations or troop costs or decisions regarding Taiwan clearly illustrate the point. Moreover, general U.S. policy toward Asia, America's relations with the communist powers, and the massive international economic difficulties besetting the great industrial noncommunist powers may well establish new frames of reference for bilateral security ties. In addition, certain assumptions must be made about American preferences in both U.S. and Japanese defense policy.

This paper assumes that the present course, with modest variations, is the one that the United States hopes to follow over the next five years or more. That is, the United States will continue to maintain a military presence in East Asia, but it will expect its allies to strengthen their own ability to cope with domestic insurrection or external attack. It will continue to provide a nuclear umbrella to allies who might be threatened by attack by a nuclear power. It will contine to regard relations with Japan as the crucial American interest in East Asia, but will seek to expand and improve relations with both China and the USSR, thus diminishing the risk of conflict in the region among the big powers.

With these purposes in mind, the following recommendations are offered to improve the likelihood of their attainment.[1]

1. The Tanaka-Nixon meeting in 1973 reassured Japan of U.S. determination to adhere to its strategic commitment to protect Japan against nuclear threat. Constant repetitions, however, will be essential in the future.[2] There will be a parallel need to demonstrate to Japan's top

1. For another general perspective, see James E. Auer, "Toward a Pacific Maritime Union: Resolving the Japan-U.S. Security Treaty Dilemma," *Pacific Community*, vol. 5 (October 1973), pp. 53–67.

2. The Tanaka-Nixon communiqué of 1973 spoke to this point in paragraph 8: "The President confirmed the intention of the United States to maintain an adequate level of deterrent forces in the region."

security officials that strategic parity between the United States and the Soviet Union means just that, not inferiority, and that such equality will in no way reduce the deterrent power of the United States. Toward this end, the United States perhaps should keep Japanese officials more fully informed of its negotiating position in the strategic arms limitation talks with the Soviet Union and of its strategic posture and contingency plans, somewhat along the lines used over the past decade to brief NATO allies.

2. Both parties might benefit from periodic meetings that center on the utility of the mutual security treaty.[3] Because the treaty is now subject to abrogation by either side with one year's notice, the establishment of a biennial review procedure might improve its durability and provide suitable occasions for the presentation of complaints and suggestions for reform. But this procedure should not preclude joint consultations to resolve specific issues as they arise.

3. The base system requires considerable rationalization and consolidation and can profit from a thorough and critical American review of the functions performed by various installations.[4] A significant cutback should be possible in Okinawa to reduce the disproportionate U.S. strength there as compared with the home islands. One economic benefit would be a saving of several hundred million dollars in U.S. balance of payments. The vexing question of major air installations requires a balance between Japanese desires for reduction and relocation and U.S. requirements for the security of its allies and the effective servicing of the carriers. One approach would be to treat air bases at Kadena and Misawa and the Yokosuka-Atsugi package in the Tokyo area as an irreducible minimum. Bargaining then could center on what to do with Sasebo and Iwakuni (because of the problems presented by the latter), whether to retain Yokota, and how many support facilities are necessary.

4. A major effort must be made to gain Japanese public support for a rationalized minimum base system. With U.S. forces out of Vietnam and U.S. relations with China improved, this may be the best time for the Japanese government to stress the vital strategic role played by the bases in maintaining the security of Japan and the overall balance of

3. A *Yomiuri* poll of June 27, 1973, found that about 55 percent favored keeping a revised mutual security treaty and that about 45 percent wanted it considerably revised or dissolved: see A. M. Halpern, "Japan: Economic Giant's Quiet Diplomacy," *International Affairs*, vol. 49 (October 1973), p. 597.

4. For a recent discussion of these issues, see Roland A. Paul, *American Military Commitments Abroad* (Rutgers University Press, 1973), chap. 4.

power in East Asia—and do so without unnecessarily increasing tensions. Both parties should drop the argument that Japan provides for its own defense, and Japan in particular should clearly depict the capabilities and limits of the Self-Defense Force in dealing with conventional military threats.

As a consequence of this approach, the Japanese people might come to realize that Japan can provide for its own security only under certain limited circumstances, and that it cannot attain autonomous defense under the existing defense effort.[5] There should be no downgrading of the value of the bases for U.S. security efforts elsewhere in the Pacific, however, since they do play a major role and the Japanese can argue rightly that the facilities represent a valid contribution to the mutuality of the security arrangement. This approach, of course, keeps the base system vulnerable to attack by the opposition, but this is inevitable.[6] A gradual and systematic consolidation of bases, indicating an honest intent to rationalize the system, is preferable to a dramatic, sweeping reduction that might weaken U.S. credibility.

5. Crucial to these arrangements is the retention of a U.S. force presence in Japan, both to resolve the very real doubts that exist in the Japan Defense Agency about American support in the event of a significant conventional attack and to reinforce the deterrent commitment against a nuclear threat. A cutback of perhaps one-third of the 27,000 troops in the home islands and a proportionally larger reduction of the 56,000 on Okinawa still could be effected, provided that both sides understood that the new levels were to be stable and reflected the smaller number of bases and installations. As noted earlier, the stationing of highly professional and disciplined troops to carry out these functions also would improve relations with the civilian population. Most essential is retention of the Seventh Fleet in Japanese waters, and the home porting of carriers at Yokosuka should be continued.

6. The retention of some U.S. combat presence in Korea is an essential related consideration. Forces there can and should be reduced substantially if the likelihood of violence diminishes on the peninsula.

5. The extent to which it is assumed that Japan does provide for its own conventional defense is exemplified in ibid., p. 50.

6. On the other hand, there is still substantial support for close links to the United States. The *Yomiuri* poll of June 1973, for example, found more respondents favoring priority relations with the United States than with any other power.

Should this occur, the U.S. Air Force units must be retained, since the Republic of Korea has a substantial ground force but cannot match North Korean air power. The retention of such a force thus helps deter a North Korean venture and also provides a balanced defense force in South Korea, without augmenting Seoul's own offensive capacity.

From an American perspective, bases in Japan and South Korea form an interlocking and mutually supporting system of air and naval power. Therefore, a reduced but still effective U.S. security presence in Northeast Asia must be able to rely on the Satō obligation of 1969: the commitment to respond affirmatively to a U.S. request for permission to deploy American forces from Japan for the defense of South Korea against an attack from the North. This undertaking should apply whether the United States operates under the UN flag or whether, should the UN presence be withdrawn, troops in Korea act solely under the auspices of the U.S.-ROK treaty.[7] On the other hand, the United States should not try to encourage Japan to take a direct interest in the security of South Korea. This would not be received favorably by the Japanese government or public, and such a policy would smack of interference. Above all, it would appear to Peking as proof of the resurrection of Japanese militarism, against which it inveighed so vigorously in the early 1970s.

Should hostility between the two Koreas continue, should Seoul overcome its deep antipathy to dependence on Japan for security, and should the Japanese become concerned about the stability of the peninsula and their ever-increasing economic investment there, the American presence could make an association between Seoul and Tokyo more feasible and palatable. But the initiative must come from the two Asian states. Currently, the American force presence in, and treaties with, both countries provide an adequate basis for regional stability—provided that the United States can deploy forces to the mainland from Japan in time of crisis.

7. The United States should be responsive to Japan's desire for policy coordination and consultation. Tokyo's long-standing interest in cabinet-level consultations should be satisfied and perhaps linked to the periodic review of the mutual security treaty conducted by the director of the Japan Defense Agency and the U.S. secretary of defense. The United States could be more responsive as well to JDA requests for more

7. The possibility of U.S. troops remaining in Korea under bilateral treaty auspices rather than under the UN command was first raised in the fall of 1973: *New York Times,* November 16, 1973.

information regarding its defense plans in East Asia. There could also be greater coordination of defense policy: in particular, contingency plans for the defense of Japan in an emergency. For example, there could be some arrangement about the availability of U.S. supply stocks to the Self-Defense Force in a crisis. In turn, the Japanese should bring their defense effort closer to the levels of preparedness called for in their own plans so that their forces could be worked more readily into joint defense plans should these come into being. Japan also could make a greater monetary contribution to the U.S. effort by paying more for base reorganization and for the maintenance of U.S. supplies, should the latter be earmarked for SDF use in time of need.

In short, the United States could be more responsive in working out coordinated efforts if Japan gave assurances that it would pull its own military and financial weight more than in the past. Japan could make this greater effort in return for access to U.S. strategic defense concepts, a role in the planning and implementation of joint defense programs, and the full cooperation of the U.S. defense force in time of crisis.

8. The United States should continue and expand its present course of cooperation with Japan in the provision of nuclear fuel and space technology. There is everything to be gained from cooperation in the peaceful uses of atomic energy, which keeps Washington informed about Japan's progress in a sensitive field and provides a critical area of cooperation in what otherwise has been the abrasive and alliance-straining problem of access to energy sources. Responsiveness in the provision of enriched uranium and joint efforts in the development of the fast-breeder reactor will increase cooperation and reduce such strains. It also could cut the costs to each nation, and perhaps hasten some solutions to the energy shortage now facing the industrial powers.

9. Cooperation in the peaceful uses of nuclear energy could give the United States additional leverage to induce Japan to ratify the nonproliferation treaty.

10. Although the United States has a considerable interest in dissuading Japan from entering the special-weapons field and should utilize positive incentives, including nuclear fuel supplies, toward this end, it should take a more passive stance regarding the further development of Japan's conventional armaments. In the past it has pursued a partially contradictory policy in this matter. On the one hand, it has constantly pressed Japan to raise its security posture to the level that the Japanese

themselves have assigned to the SDF in their formal defense missions. These efforts have aroused resentment and should be muted.[8]

At the same time, Washington has demonstrated unhappiness, primarily for balance-of-payments reasons, about Tokyo's efforts to reduce purchases from the United States and to augment its technological self-sufficiency in modern conventional armaments. Though this orientation reduces the combat readiness of the SDF, it does stimulate a heretofore inadequate defense effort and to a degree increases Japan's preparedness. Because the Japanese continue to rely on the United States for expensive and sophisticated conventional items, American interests still are adequately served with regard both to sales to Japan and to monitoring of the country's defense effort. This relation also retains the link among the elite in technological fields, which is all the more important now that military training programs for Japanese soldiers in the United States have been terminated. Some responsiveness in advanced technical aspects of conventional weapons would strengthen this important connection, increase U.S. sales, and reinforce Japan's inclination to turn to the United States for new, expensive items that lie on the frontiers of its technological capability and not to produce them itself.

8. According to the *Yomiuri* poll of June 1973, a substantial minority believed that the United States would carry out its security obligations, but a greater number saw the United States as demanding that Japan assume those obligations. On the other hand, the Japanese are interested in developing a larger capability against the submarine danger: *New York Times*, November 25, 1973.